Reading between the lines
Teacher's Book

Reading between the lines

Integrated language and
literature activities

Teacher's Book

*John McRae and
Roy Boardman*

CAMBRIDGE
UNIVERSITY PRESS

PUBLISHED BY THE PRESS SYNDICATE OF THE UNIVERSITY OF CAMBRIDGE
The Pitt Building, Trumpington Street, Cambridge CB2 1RP, United Kingdom

CAMBRIDGE UNIVERSITY PRESS
The Edinburgh Building, Cambridge CB2 2RU, UK http://www.cup.cam.ac.uk
40 West 20th Street, New York, NY 10011–4211, USA http://www.cup.org
10 Stamford Road, Oakleigh, Melbourne 3166, Australia

© Cambridge University Press 1984

First published 1984
Seventh printing 1998

Printed in the United Kingdom at the University Press, Cambridge

Library of Congress catalogue card number: 84—4262

British Library cataloguing in publication data

McRae, John
Reading between the lines.
Teacher's book
1. English language — Text-books for foreign
speakers
I. Title   II. Boardman, Roy
428.2'4   P1128

ISBN 0 521 27790 6 Teacher's Book
ISBN 0 521 27789 2 Student's Book
ISBN 0 521 25992 4 Set of 2 cassettes

MU

Contents

Thanks   vi

Introduction   1
The language focus   4
The literature focus   7
Conclusion   8
Some dos and don'ts about using this book   9

1 Family   10

2 Environment   18

3 War   24

4 Women   31

5 Authority   40

6 Indifference   45

7 Rebellion   51

8 Ideals   59

9 Ambitions   67

10 Meaning   74

Appendix: The authors   81

Thanks

We would like to thank all those dedicated Italian teachers who have worked closely and consistently with us on these materials over many years. Special thanks are due to Jeremy Hunter for seeing the typescript through its several versions.

J M
R B

Introduction

Reading between the lines is for upper intermediate and more advanced students of English as a foreign language. It has two main aims:

1 To improve and develop students' *understanding and use of the language* through the reading and discussion of literary texts.
2 To awaken students' appreciative and critical faculties and so encourage their *development as readers of literature.*

We do not see these aims as distinct: it is our conviction that the intermediate/advanced foreign-language learner should, and usually wishes to, progress to the reading of literature, while it is also true that literature makes an irreplaceable contribution to the development of communicative competence. In this definition of the place of literature in the teaching of English as a foreign language, *the ability to read literary texts with pleasure and understanding is a fundamental component of that communicative competence of the educated native speaker which is the final goal of foreign students and their teachers.*

The structure of each of the ten theme-based units reflects this double aim.

STRUCTURE	EXAMPLE
Unit	**Unit One**
Quotation (from a unit text)	*We're a family, aren't we?*
Stage 1 Theme	
A preliminary fluency activity involving a combination of reading, listening, writing and predominantly speaking. The activity is designed to: – raise awareness of the unit theme – relate it to the individual feelings, opinions and experiences of the students – initiate the exchange of students' feelings, opinions and experiences	Song: Cat Stevens, 'Father and Son'. Recording. Visuals. Group work, leading to class discussion on family problems, especially parent-child relationships and how problems might differ from country to country. Students make notes on the outcome of the discussion.

STRUCTURE	EXAMPLE
– provide opportunities for the recall of relevant language – by means of all these, prepare the way for the literary texts Various stimuli are used in Stage 1: songs, visuals, quotations, short texts illustrating different or contrasting aspects of the theme.	
Stage 2 Text A The first literary text, which the reading incentives, questions, pair and group activities help to place in the context of students' feelings, opinions and experiences. The student receives the writer's contribution to the theme almost as he or she receives fellow students' contributions. The student is also encouraged to examine the writer's special use of language, though most work is generally reserved for later.	From *Sons and Lovers* by D.H. Lawrence. – Family outsiders, hating and loving one's parents in adolescence. – Paragraph construction, effect of past-tense narration, character descriptions (contrast with Dickens, *Hard Times*).
Stage 3 Text B At this stage there is sometimes only one text and the more literary questions are introduced at Stage 4. This text extends and deepens responses to the theme. The relationship between text and students' feelings, opinions and experiences is maintained.	From *Chicken Soup with Barley* by Arnold Wesker. Family relationships, different attitudes of sons and daughters, characters and roles of fathers and mothers.
Text C With the third text, it becomes fruitful to compare and contrast ways in which the authors present their themes. Close reading, analysis and discussion take a more literary turn; the emphasis is on the way writers use language to convey their meanings.	From *A Night Out* by Harold Pinter. Interpreting stage directions, functions of stage directions.

Stage 4 Text D	
A further text sharpens the literary focus at this point in most units (with the exception of Units 2 and 9).	From *Emma* by Jane Austen. Understatement, irony (*Does Jane Austen's way of writing about family difficulties make it easy, or difficult, to identify them?*).
Stage 5 Simulation	
The simulation is a means by which the ideas, feelings and viewpoints that the students have derived from the unit can be assembled and put to a specific use, so providing fluency practice. Each simulation has a written product – a letter, a report, etc.	Students simulate aspiring social workers. The object of the simulation is to write to the Social Services Authority about careers in family advice centres.
Stage 6 Language	
The presence of several texts on related themes gives rise to an interesting general language point. Students return to the texts in their investigation of this language point and produce passages or notes as a way of focusing attention on it.	– Communication through, without and in spite of *dialogue*. – Students write notes on a possible dialogue between Mr Woodhouse and his daughter in the Jane Austen passage, which has no dialogue.
POSTSCRIPT	
The postscripts to each unit show that discussion of the theme could go on and on; sometimes they will open up new areas for talk, or for written work. They show that there can be no simple 'conclusions' to draw. The Teacher's Book deliberately makes no comment on the Postscript texts.	*All happy families resemble one another, each unhappy family is unhappy in its own way.* Leo Tolstoy, *Anna Karenina*

Translated into terms of 1½ – 2 hour lessons, we have found that the following scheme, as long as it is used flexibly, works well in practice.

Lesson 1 Stages 1 and 2. It is occasionally advisable, however, to spend a whole lesson on Stage 1.

3

Lesson 2   Stage 3. There are times, for example in Unit 7, when this will become two lessons on account of the sharper literary focus and increased difficulty.

Lesson 3   Stage 4. The increased literary focus makes it worth giving a whole lesson to this stage. Include preparation for Stage 5, the simulation, either in class or as homework.

Lesson 4   Stages 5 and 6. When necessary, the re-reading and written work at Stage 6 can be done at home.

This general scheme makes the book suitable for a wide range of teaching/learning situations. Classes using it might or might not be going on to a formal study of literature, they might or might not have commenced work on set books. Whatever the situation, the scheme ensures that the two complementary aims remain sides of the same coin, though the teacher may decide to focus on one of them.

The language focus

The teacher may decide to focus on improving and developing the class's understanding and use of the *language*. It is self-evident that exposure to literary texts will increase sensitivity to language; we assume, however, that students need guidance in their *interaction with the texts*. Reading literature differs fundamentally from reading anything else in that the relationship that normally holds between the text and the real world is absent: the writer invents it as he or she goes along, and the reader is required to invent it again for him or herself. An aspect of the real world that must come into play, however, in relation to this re-invention, is the reader's self: the *set* of his or her experience, opinions, feelings, aspirations and so on. In the interpretation of literary texts, the writer's set (as manifested in the text itself) and the reader's set are pitted against each other so that such things as whether or not an experience is shared by author and reader, whether the reader believes that a specific attitude of mind is possible or acceptable, whether he or she is capable of feeling a particular emotion, acquire great importance. It is for this reason that *Reading between the lines* provides plentiful opportunities for students to share feelings and opinions, to recount individual experiences, and to bring these to bear on the texts. Where we expect this to happen, and where, therefore, we cannot suggest what the content of student responses might be, this Teacher's Book uses the term 'open response'.

The kind of language practice that *Reading between the lines* provides is *fluency practice*. Students are not expected, in any particular activity, to produce language in predetermined patterns; they are not required to select from any restricted area of syntax, vocabulary, communicative functions and so on – all that matters is the degree of success with which they convey, in speech or writing, what they mean.

Fluency practice of the kind you will find in this book is, in our view, essential to the foreign language student's learning. There are many reasons why this is so, of which the following four are fundamental.

1 Students need the challenge of having to call on the whole range of language they have learnt in attempting to convey specific meanings.

2 Where the language needed to express a particular meaning is not available, the student, like the native speaker, has to 'invent' language – hence the occurrence of neologism and metaphor, for example. Only fluency practice activities offer this possibility.

3 In effective and interesting speech and writing, the user ranges from specific to general, and this variety greatly facilitates communication. Statements are accompanied by examples, evidence is presented to back up opinions, systems of belief are related to the palpable world. *Reading between the lines* not only gives ample opportunity to vary expression in this way, but also actively encourages it by asking for examples, evidence and the relating of abstractions to things experienced.

4 Language is generally no better than the speaker's or writer's understanding of the situation. The extensive use that fluency practice makes possible, together with the reading and other related activities that prepare for such practice, assist the development of such understanding. As the student progresses through a unit, his or her thinking and feeling about the topic is deepened and enriched, making for more effective personal expression.

Look at this example of a typical group activity from *Reading between the lines*, in which the students pit their own experiences of family life against the presentation of an aspect of family life in Lawrence's *Sons and Lovers*. The following questions precede the text and guide the student's reading of it:

a) Why is the father an outsider in the home?
b) How old is Paul?
c) What does Paul dislike most about his father?
d) Can we ever see a positive side to the father's nature?

The instructions for the paired discussion follow the text as follows:

Discuss the answers you have found to the questions, before going on, and, if you wish, relate each one to your personal experience of family life by talking about the following points with a partner. The letters (a) to (d) relate the points to the questions you have answered.

a) Think of an outsider in your own family, or in a family you know well. What is his/her influence on family life?

b) Is it common at Paul's age for young people to feel they hate their fathers and mothers, or conversely have a very strong attachment to them?

c) Have *you* ever felt strong dislike for a parent's behaviour or attitudes? What attitudes does the son dislike in Cat Stevens's song?

d) What are the positive sides of *your own* nature, do you think, from the point of view of other members of your family?

We firmly believe that the more frequent the fluency practice, the greater the possibility of observable success in language learning – whether the teacher is present to monitor such practice or not. In *Reading between the lines*, the content of fluency practice activities is very personal; students are given opportunities to express what they feel and think about matters they really care about.

Towards the end of each unit, students have delved deep into the topic: they have examined their own attitudes towards it, they have been exposed to the attitudes of writers and of fellow students, and they have perhaps developed new attitudes of their own. It is useful at this point to get them to look back at all this in a single activity. This is the purpose of the *simulation* in each unit; the class's thoughts, feelings and conflicting attitudes are gathered together for a purpose, in order to perform a specific task. The task is a double one, providing fluency practice in both speech and writing.

The improvement in students' language use to which *Reading between the lines* will contribute is brought about, however, not only by constant practice, but also by constant *evaluation of language use*. The language of the texts, which is regarded as language used for real communicative purposes, is being examined all the time, while the final activity of each unit draws attention to some generalisation: the language of contrast, simile and metaphor, sexist language, and so on.

To summarise, *Reading between the lines* brings about an improvement in the student's use of English by:
a) exposure to a wide range of texts;
b) extensive fluency practice;
c) reflection on the language.

The literature focus

The teacher may decide to focus on the awakening of students' appreciative and critical faculties in order to encourage their development as *readers of literature.*

The 'set books' which are normally part, if not the whole, of the literature syllabus cannot offer a sufficient range of literary expression for the achievement of this aim; while *Reading between the lines offers a wide range of forms, styles, periods and authors.*

The 'outline of literature' approach, with its emphasis on history, movements, the personal details of authors, influence, and so on, and its neglect of textual study, has even less to contribute to the student's development as a reader of literature; whereas *Reading between the lines is based on the reading of texts.*

The approach through literary criticism, with its comparison of methods of analysis and of conflicting evaluations, is at its best dependent on the student's direct knowledge of the texts under discussion and therefore on his or her previously-acquired literary competence; *Reading between the lines does not assume such competence – on the contrary, it aims at helping students to acquire it.*

In its concentration on the texts themselves, the book gets students to look at the ways in which literature uses language for specific ends; it therefore directs attention at familiar processes such as lexical selection and syntactic variety, as well as more specifically literary devices – rhyme, rhythm, deviations from the norm, modes of character and scene presentation, to name but a few.

The texts have been selected *not* in consideration of their literary 'importance', but because of:
– their contribution to a particular non-literary theme;
– their inherent interest;
– the language features they incorporate;
– their ability to stand alone, cut off from the works of which they are part, as 'communicative acts'.

Introduction

A further consideration has been the need to present a comprehensive range of kinds and levels of difficulty, and a number of the activities are designed to assist students to acquire the skills needed to tackle such difficulties: see Unit 7 Text B, for example, on Milton's *Paradise Lost*, Unit 9 Text C on Gray's *Elegy Written in a Country Churchyard*, and Unit 6 Text E on Dylan Thomas's *A Refusal to Mourn*.

The texts have been ordered according to topic. Contemporary texts are mixed with older works so that you will find a living novelist rubbing shoulders with a seventeenth-century poet. This arrangement adds variety, enriches the topic approach, and helps to highlight stylistic variation.

The recordings

The recordings on the cassettes should not, if the book is to achieve what it sets out to achieve, be considered optional. *Listening to literature* is pleasurable, illuminating and appropriate; it has, of course, little to do with practical listening skills, but everything to do with an added dimension in the interpretation of texts. Advice on the use of specific recordings is given in the unit notes.

For copyright reasons it was not possible to publish every single text on cassette. However, most of the texts are recorded and are indicated in both the Student's and Teacher's Books by the symbol ▭ .

Conclusion

Although you, the teacher, might be interested in one or the other focus, language or literature, you must remember that a different focus does not entail a different way of using the book. The language-literature aims are, we repeat, complementary, the book has been organised to make them so, and you cannot achieve one without achieving the other. Whichever focus you decide on, the following order of work on the units is recommended:

Unit 1   First
Unit 2
Unit 3
Unit 4   After Unit 1 and before Units 8, 9, 10 but
Unit 5   *in any order.*
Unit 6
Unit 7

8

Unit 8 } After Units 1 – 7
Unit 9 }
Unit 10 Last

The teacher's notes on each unit provide a running commentary including suggested answers to questions, background information, and advice on methodology and teaching techniques. Brief information on all the authors included in *Reading between the lines*, for you to use as you wish, appears in the appendix.

Before you begin preparing your first lesson and reading the unit notes, we suggest you read the Dos and Don'ts that follow.

Some dos and don'ts about using this book

DO	DON'T
remember literature is language	be put off because a text seems difficult; the questions and activities are designed to help come to grips with it
bring out the students' own experience	
encourage students to evaluate texts in relation to themselves – this is the first step on the way to critical appreciation	impose your own ideas; nor, however, keep your ideas too much to yourself
trust the questions and activities to help you	think of literature as having a capital L
allow your own experience and feelings to emerge; relate the texts to yourself too	feel you have to do every unit, or every text in the units you do
encourage students to find out for themselves about authors / texts / historical background, etc.	be afraid to dislike a text
	expect your students to like every text and every activity
be prepared for all kinds of reaction to the texts!	
enjoy the book – reading should be a pleasure; your enjoyment will communicate itself to the students	
use the cassettes	

9

1 Family

We're a family, aren't we?

The book begins with a topic to which every student can
contribute. Everyone has a family, and no family is perfect.
Students are encouraged to compare their family experiences
and their feelings with each other and with the characters in the
texts. It will help students to get to know each other and to
become accustomed to the idea of referring texts to their own
experience.

1.1 Theme 🔲

The song shows some aspects of the so-called 'generation gap'.
Students will probably have had similar experiences of
unwanted or irrelevant advice from parents. The son wants to
leave – quite simply he has had enough of being 'ordered to
listen'.

Elicit similar feelings. Have students ever felt like running
away from home? Who is right? Is there right and wrong in the
matter? Can we have sympathy with the father? Do students
ever feel as alone as the son does?

The first two points of the unit show how exchange of
experiences, opinions and ideas takes place in *Reading between
the lines*. The discussion in 1.1 is done in pairs while 1.2 enables
students to pool the results of discussion and provides an
opportunity for each individual to select what he finds most
interesting and/or relevant.

It is advisable, during pair, group and class discussion, to
avoid interrupting with language comments and corrections.
Help students to convey their meanings, by all means, but foster
the importance of content.

1.2 Experiences of family life always differ from individual to
individual, but we must also remember that relationships within
the family, and family traditions, vary enormously from country
to country. If your class is a monolingual group, the discussion
will mainly hinge on the contrasts between family life in the

10

students' own country, and British family life as represented by the teacher and/or texts. Discussion will be much fuller, of course, with multilingual groups.

2.1 Text A D.H. Lawrence, *Sons and Lovers*

PROCEDURE
i)   Students listen to the recording and follow the text.
ii)   They read the pre-reading questions.
iii) They read the text silently, looking for evidence which will suggest answers to the questions.
iv)   They talk about their answers with a partner. The four points (a) to (d) which follow the text are 'open response' aspects of the matters raised by the comprehension questions, and explicitly encourage students to relate text to personal feelings, opinions and experiences. Point out that comprehension question (a) couples with open response question (a), etc.

VOCABULARY POINTS
Dialect: 'I'll lay my fist about thy y'ead', etc. The use of 'thee/ thou' (second person) is still quite common in some Northern, Midland, and Western dialects in England. This passage uses Nottinghamshire/Derbyshire dialect. Dialect will, of course, be found recurrently throughout the book, especially in texts from earlier periods.
whoam   home
doesna/dost   don't / do you
the scotch   (a rare expression, its meaning is relatively clear) the only interruption or negative factor
as   that (l.39)
cobbled   repaired (only of footwear) (cf. cobbler)
pit-bottle   in which he took water to the pit to drink while at work
iron goose   a kind of small anvil
moleskin   not real moleskin, but a smooth fabric resembling it

COMPREHENSION QUESTIONS
a)   Because he spends the day away from home, in another world, down the mine, and when he comes home he finds difficulty in adjusting to this other world. As a result he reacts violently, is left alone, excluded and feared.
b)   The chapter 'The Young Life of Paul' does not give Paul's age, but students will imagine he is in his early teens.

c) Probably his bullying (cf. 'he was dangerous' (l.3), and the fifth paragraph, from l.15).

d) Yes, when he is working at home.

2.2
a) First, some understanding is shown at 'He would dearly have liked the children to talk to him'. This is built upon in the conversation that follows. The whole description of the father cobbling, soldering etc. gives a more sympathetic insight into his character, showing him in a creative, absorbed attitude, in complete contrast with the rest of the passage.

b) Other words used to refer to Mr Morel, 'his father': he / the collier / the man / the father / your father / Morel. The frequent changes make us wonder about his identity within the family – the 'outsider' effect is strengthened.

c) Because (as in 2.1a) he feels excluded, uncomfortable, not a real part of the home. He realises the situation is a difficult one. Whether he fully realises what the others think of him is debatable.

d) This question leaves a lot of room for discussion. It is clearly not a particularly satisfactory relationship. Useful guiding vocabulary: one-sided, lacking communication, acceptance, rejection, tolerance.

e) Open response.

f) Open response.

2.3   The narrative flows easily from one paragraph to another, and the smooth transition from one aspect of the theme to another is achieved by the simplest of means. 'And' and 'Then' give the piece an almost biblical tone.

The passage is about *people*, and people are kept in focus by constant reference to them at the beginnings of the paragraphs (Paul, Morel, personal pronouns). The one-line, single-sentence paragraphs in the conversation between Paul and his father emphasise the awkwardness of the relationship. The final paragraph is longer than the others, and the sentences which make it up are also generally longer, to bring out the contrast in its content. Morel is relaxed, happy, satisfied, and the description of him working is relaxed too. Notice that its sentences are again linked very simply.

2.4 a) The 'used to' meaning applies from the beginning of the passage to 'You ought to tell your father'. The other meaning of the past tense, for events that occurred only once, is found only in the scene about Paul's prize, from 'Paul won a prize...' to 'And that was all'. This is a very isolated event, but made in this distancing way to appear symptomatic of the Paul/father relationship.

b) 'Sometimes Mrs Morel would say...' makes explicit the idea of regular occurrence over a period of time, before the account of the one-off conversation between Paul and his father. The sentence that follows 'And that was all', 'Conversation was impossible...', effects a natural transition from the 'one-off' meaning to the regular-occurrence meaning of the past tense.

2.5 a) Open response. One example the students give might be 'paltry', stressing Paul's hatred of the smallness of his father's brows. Other suggestions: shouted, brutal, shut out, And that was all, etc.

b) Students might pick on:
   – The grotesque humour of the figurative language in the Dickens passage, compared with the serious realism of Lawrence's piece;
   – Dickens's use of repeated syntax and vocabulary ('The emphasis') giving a forceful rhythm to the piece which builds up relentlessly, compared with Lawrence's single sentences. The recording brings out the rhythm.

   Dickens ridicules his character, wants us to laugh at him; Lawrence is expressing the family's, especially Paul's, attitude to Morel.

3.1 **Text B** Arnold Wesker, *Chicken Soup with Barley*

Harry and Sarah are Ada and Ronnie's parents.

VOCABULARY POINTS
'*Ach*' is a typical Jewish ejaculation. The rhythms of the dialogue are Jewish.
up West   to the West End of London, the entertainment district
solo   a card game
Hymie and Lottie   typical Jewish names, short for Hiram and Charlotte
form master   teacher in charge of a class at school

13

Family

COMPREHENSION QUESTIONS
a) Students may decide for themselves. Actually Ada is 24, Ronnie is about 15.
b) Ada in a two-room flat, Ronnie with their parents.
c) Her excuse is that she has 'to write a letter' and so on, but we imagine she leaves to escape the family argument.
d) He is Ada's husband. (He has been away for six years in the war. The scene is set in 1946.)
e) Ada wants to escape, Ronnie accepts and tries to make peace. This is possibly because Ada is older, more used to family quarrels and less prepared to tolerate them. Ronnie wants peace because he has to live in the same house as his parents.
f) Sarah is dramatising the situation for anybody who will listen (and even if nobody is listening), in order to vent her own frustrations and torment Harry the more.
g) Useful guiding vocabulary: strained, vindictive, tense, etc. Is *either* strong? Students will probably think Sarah the stronger.
h) Open response.

3.2   Open response.

4.1   Text C   Harold Pinter, *A Night Out* 📼

Both mothers try to be domineering. They are very demanding, almost martyrs. Albert's mother is more limited, simply because she only has Albert to complain to.
a) He is 28. (The passage does not state his age.)
b) An office job. The company is later identified as Hislop, King and Martindale, but its business is never revealed.
c) Colleagues of Albert's.
d) It seems not.
e) Yes – he seems to be used to handling his mother's demands.
f) No, he would not. He says it to placate her.
g) Game of cards / the bulb / I told you yesterday / You don't expect me... / Your father... / You're all I've got... (climax).
h) She is possessive because she has no one else, is selfish, and is afraid of being left alone.

4.2 a) The first two pauses give Albert's mother time to prepare her elements of emotional blackmail, and also keep Albert in suspense and probably some embarrassment. The third follows mother's strongest attempt at blackmail, and Albert has no answer to it – his only possibility is to leave. Mother pauses during her lines for emotional effect (slight sobs or intakes of breath). So it is probably deliberate; it is therefore unlikely that she is at a loss for words.

b) With one exception, all the stage directions fall into these categories. The exception is '*He is having his first stroke*', which gives information to the actors and the director or to the reader, which allow them to decide on Harry's behaviour and Sarah's reaction. Wesker uses many more stage directions than Pinter, and many of them describe tones of voice. Pinter uses them very sparingly, and occasionally when lines are open to misinterpretation (such as *Touching her breast* to clarify 'In here! And this is his house!').

4.3 Open response.

5.1 **Text D** Jane Austen, *Emma*

Note: In the original text the doctors are called 'Mr'. We have adopted the more modern usage for the sake of clarity.

There is perhaps a little criticism of Mrs John Knightley in lines 35-36; and also the remark about Mr John Knightley's temper (ll.48-49), which leads to the final, slightly uncomfortable observations, showing that the seemingly perfect relationship does have its flaws. Of course, the difficulties here are minimal compared to the other families. Discussion might centre on whether difficulties beginning with such seemingly small differences could create a progressively worse family atmosphere.

5.2 Open response. The exercise has two purposes: to get students to review all the texts in the unit in preparation for 6 and 7; and to get them to produce summaries of links between the content of the texts and personal experiences and attitudes.

6 Simulation

Recommended duration: 1 hour 15 minutes

In each of the simulations, students pretend to be in a situation requiring the performance of specific tasks, both oral and written. Their satisfactory performance is dependent on much of the work that has been done on the unit: the reading, discussion, individual explorations into personal experience and attitudes.

The distinction between tasks to be carried out individually, in pairs, and in groups is crucial. You may, however, vary the size of the groups to suit your classes.

In this simulation, we suggest that:

a) is done in the group of four or five;
b) is partly individual, but students may wish to exchange ideas on books;
c) must be done in the group;
d) is both individual and in the group;
e) gets groups interacting.

Make absolutely sure that students know exactly what you expect of them at each stage, and set time limits throughout. For later simulations some of the preparatory and written work can be done at home, but we recommend that the whole of this first one is performed in the classroom. Much depends on students' previous experience of simulations, role plays, and working in groups; the *Reading between the lines* simulations, however, are rather different from anything they will have experienced before, so it is a good idea to devote a whole lesson to the first one. The final product of each of the simulations is a piece of written work. There are instructions concerned with students reading each other's work, a step never to be missed.

7 Dialogue

a) The questions raise the problems of non-communication in dialogue: Father and Son are not communicating in the song; Paul's father reaches a level of communication with his children when he is working at home – so what does the dialogue reveal and what does it hide? It should emerge that dialogue often covers an inability to communicate meaning-fully. The play excerpts show undercurrents of feeling which are expressed in action (Ronnie's doing the washing-up) or inaction (Albert's mother's pauses).

b) Note that students are *not* asked to write a dialogue, but to explore what such a dialogue might be like, in order to draw attention to the possibilities of dialogue as a device (direct speech) as against narration (indirect speech).

The students should concentrate on Mr Woodhouse's worries and Mrs John Knightley's reassurances. It will emerge that the style of such a dialogue would be rather formal and polite in contrast with the very modern conversational style of the play excerpts. This might lead to a discussion of the advantages and disadvantages of very formal conversation, and of the conventions imposed on it. Conversational conventions such as calling people by their names, pet names, formal titles, or short forms, or allusions to shared knowledge, can be discussed. How would students address a fellow student, a teacher, their headmaster, and so on?

POSTSCRIPT

All happy families resemble one another, each unhappy family is unhappy in its own way.

Leo Tolstoy, *Anna Karenina*

2 Environment

It isn't going to last.

This unit shows the continuing nature of environmental problems and is designed to bring out students' reactions to them in relation to the attitudes of writers of very different periods: William Cowper (18th century) and Philip Larkin (20th century). In the third passage, from Konrad Lorenz's *Civilized Man's Eight Deadly Sins*, the problems are strongly felt and expressed very directly – an alternative means of expression brought out in 4.3(a).

Students might need some relevant vocabulary which you can give or elicit during 1: neglect, pollution, speculation, preservation, conservation, and so on.

1 Theme

Open response. The contrast is between 'There is nothing there' (It doesn't matter) and a caring attitude. Elicit where students' sympathies lie, and why. (e) sets the problem of the 'other passengers on this planet with us' – plants, insects, animals, etc. These would be the 'specific losses', and the photograph will help you. Students could prepare 'for and against' arguments if there are different opinions in the class. This is preparatory to the reading of *The Ecologist* manifesto. You might wish to note in passing the matter-of-fact, unliterary style of the text which will later be in contrast to the poetry texts in this unit. Elicit which side it appears to be on (clearly against the chopping down of the forests), and whether it convinces the supporters of the destruction policy.

2.1 Text A William Cowper, *The Poplar Field* 📼

a) and b) A set of dictionaries should be made available. However, students will need access to more than the usual language-learning dictionaries, for example to the *Shorter Oxford English Dictionary*.

c) They are 'poetic' mainly because they are structured

to provide rhymes at the ends of the lines, and to scan. In general, contemporary poetry does not alter so radically the sentence structures of everyday speech and writing: an important point, given the contrast with Larkin's poem.

d) This will highlight points such as the position of 'no longer', the use of 'nor' and 'behold', and the general matter of lexical-syntactic relationships.

2.2 Language Cowper uses to express the past-present contrast: farewell – no longer – elapsed since – last – now – once – before – no more

Language students might use in expressing the contrasts, which provide a summary of the main content of the poem:

a) The poplars that used to grow along the River Ouse have been cut down.
b) You used to be able to see their reflection in the water, but now there is nothing to see. Their reflection is no longer there.
c) Cowper once used to sit under the trees. Now he sits *on* them. The trees are no longer standing.
d) He used to hear the blackbirds singing. Now they have flown away. The blackbirds are no longer there.
e) Cowper used to be as strong and alive as the poplars. Now he thinks he will die soon.

2.3
a) encourages the use of more language to express past-present contrasts.
b) makes students aware of personal attitudes and opinions which help in responding to the Larkin poem.

2.4 Students relate the unit topic, and Cowper's experience in particular, to personal experience. The exercise is a written one to give students time for reflection, and as a culmination to the first major part of the unit. On completion of the exercise, they will be particularly receptive to Larkin's poem.

3.1 Text B Philip Larkin, *Going, Going*

This poem was commissioned by the Department of the Environment and it first appeared in 1972 in *How do you want to live?* For the idea of auctions in the title see answer 3.4(h).

a) Open response, preparatory to handling specific questions.
b) *split-level shopping*   a shopping area on different levels
   bleak high-risers   skyscrapers which are rather depressing
      to look at and live in
   takeover bid   an offer to buy a majority shareholding in
      a company, and thus have a controlling interest in it
   M1 café (l.20)   an eating-place on the motorway (M stands
      for motorway – the M1 connects London with the
      North)
   the Business Page (l.24)   the part of a newspaper dealing
      with finance
   slum (l.41)   a building development in very poor condition

3.2 a) Withdraws, with an implication of defeat in the face of the
         high-risers, or fear of them.
      b) Interfere with it, play around carelessly with it.
      c) Die.
      d) The whole thing, everything.
      e) (The slum is) populated (like a play) by criminals, prostitutes
         and undesirables, who have lowered the tone of the place
         morally as well as physically.

3.3 a) Cowper uses the negative presence of what used to be: the f
         sounds of line 1 begin the note of loss which is elaborated
         through negatives – 'no longer' (l.3), 'Nor' (l.4) – until the
         full loss is described in line 8.
            Larkin 'thought' (l.1) everything would be all right. He
         describes the encroachment of new buildings (l.11), and
         trees being cut down (l.5), but in terms of what remains
         rather than what is lost. He goes on to show that this
         complacency was mistaken.
      b) Cowper says that 'I see' (l.19) that such a sentiment is
         misplaced – man's 'enjoyments' (l.19) are 'less durable even
         than he' (l.20). This contradicts Larkin's line, as Larkin
         himself goes on to do.
      c) Cowper in lines 14 and 15 imagines himself in his grave,
         lying like the felled trees, in a graveyard, before new trees
         can have time to grow to replace the ones he now sees felled.
         Larkin treats his death lightly ('before I snuff it' (l.38)), less
         romantically than Cowper, but with a more urgent sense of
         time passing. Cowper's poem is imbued with a concern for
         death that is more personal than social.
      d) The building of concrete jungles threatens, such that 'The

shadows, the meadows, the lanes' (l.45) will only remain in books and pictures (and works like these two poems). Cowper reflects on an incident and its implications rather than on a continuing, expanding problem, which is just what Larkin describes. Both are personal in their commitment, but Cowper muses on 'the perishing pleasures of man' (l.18) in a rather less anxious tone than Larkin. Both want us to reflect on personal as well as universal or social loss.

3.4 a) The problem is basically the same: the threat to the countryside and to the natural world by the spread of city life, technical life, 'progress'. Cowper's problem, almost two centuries before Larkin, was rather less pressing than Larkin's.

b) The problem is not a local one, so Larkin cannot limit himself as Cowper does. Cowper is using the destruction to reflect on the durability of life and nature, rather than on a pressing social problem: for him the problem had not reached the proportions it had by 1972, although the basic concern is the same.

c) Similarities might be found in:

Cowper	ll.5–6	Larkin	ll.4–5
Cowper	ll.13–17	Larkin	ll.33–38
Cowper	ll.9–12	Larkin	l.45

Differences might be found more in general than in particular lines.

d) Contrast Cowper's 'cool colonnade' (l.2) with Larkin's 'bleak high-risers' (l.11) and 'the whole Boiling' (ll.38–39), Cowper's l.3 with Larkin's ll.4-5, Cowper's ll.18–20 with Larkin's ll.14–15, Cowper's 'Ere' (l.16) with Larkin's 'before' (l.38), and others – 'Or' (l.19), 'isn't' (l.37), 'won't' (ll.42,51), etc.

e), f) and g) Discussion will tend to make answers and comments on these questions overlap.

Cowper's rhythm and rhymes (a a b b) are simpler and more obvious. Larkin's a b c a b c is belied by his colloquial turns of phrase and run-on lines (ll.7–8, for example). The discussion of how successful rhyme is is always subjective: is the message conveyed more effectively with the order which rhyme imposes, or not? The discussion will bring out students' expectations of poetry, and whether the message contained in a poem is more readily accepted when the form conforms to the reader's idea of what a poem should be. Differences in period create different expectations. Cowper's style is more formal and ordered. Larkin's is very carefully ordered too, but appears less so because of the close resemblance to everyday speech and writing. Many students will prefer Larkin's poem as seemingly less formal – art concealing art, in fact.

h) Larkin's sentence ending 'in summer' is left suspended because we know very well how it should end – with some such phrase as 'we all know what we'll find, don't we?' It is like one speaker finishing what he is saying, and the conversation being picked up by the second speaker with 'It seems, just now...'.

Cowper expresses the situation fully, without relating fully his musings 'on the perishing pleasures of man' (l.18). This perhaps allows the reader himself to reflect on the same subject.

The title stops before 'Gone' because things have not quite got that bad – but they are two-thirds of the way there! 'Going, Going, Gone' is the standard phrase used by an auctioneer when all bids have been made and the sale is completed. Larkin applies the 'formula' phrase to a different kind of 'going'.

4.1 Text C Konrad Lorenz, *Civilized Man's Eight Deadly Sins*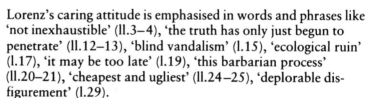

Lorenz's caring attitude is emphasised in words and phrases like 'not inexhaustible' (ll.3–4), 'the truth has only just begun to penetrate' (ll.12–13), 'blind vandalism' (l.15), 'ecological ruin' (l.17), 'it may be too late' (l.19), 'this barbarian process' (ll.20–21), 'cheapest and ugliest' (ll.24–25), 'deplorable disfigurement' (l.29).

4.2 Open response. Discuss how destruction of the landscape affects mankind. Is nature necessary to man's well-being? What are the advantages of urbanisation? What do students enjoy in nature? What would they miss most if nature were lost? What would be the worst crime of those mentioned in the unit?

4.3 a) Open response.
b) Lorenz's piece is obviously addressed to a wide reading

public, and his purpose is to convince them and alert them to danger. Larkin is talking to himself as well as to the reading public, and the fact that he sees himself as addressing the public is made overt: 'We can always escape in the car' / 'Things are tougher than we are' / 'all that remains For us', etc.

5 Simulation

Recommended duration: (a) and (b)   20 minutes
(c)   30 minutes
(d)   25 minutes
Total   1 hour 15 minutes

During the class discussion (c), students will need to take notes. Stage (d) may be done in class or for homework.

6 Contrast

a) The present-past contrasts of Larkin's poem are much more subtly expressed than Cowper's, especially because those in Cowper describe *unexpected* change; Larkin describes a gradual and inevitable development that is present from the very beginning ('I thought it would last my time' / 'Such trees as were not cut down' / 'some Have always been left so far'). The other main contrast in *Going, Going* occurs in line 18 '– But what do I feel now? Doubt?' In the Lorenz passage, students will search for more obviously linguistic expressions of contrast: Nevertheless / but / Least of all / No wonder.

b) It is useful to provide students with models of the varieties of text, if they can be made available. If you are doubtful about your students' ability to approximate sufficiently well to the varieties, advise them to select the first, a newspaper article, as this will be the most familiar.

POSTSCRIPT

Men have an extraordinarily erroneous opinion of their position in nature, and the error is ineradicable.

W. Somerset Maugham, *A Writer's Notebook*

3 War

A very nasty outbreak of peace.

If you were to ask your students which of the topics in *Reading between the lines* they would prefer to discuss, *war* would be requested by very few. Once they work their way into the unit, however, you will find them extremely responsive; they are interested in finding many facets to a theme which in general discussion, or in everyday reactions to news items, for example, gets such black-and-white treatment.

The preliminary extracts to stimulate talk, by Frederick Forsyth and Thucydides, are twenty-three centuries apart, and the other texts in the unit, ranging from Shakespeare to Wilfred Owen and Winston Churchill, illustrate the changing nature of, and attitudes to, war – while the violence and extremes it produces remain constant.

1.1 Theme

The Forsyth and Thucydides texts bring out a spectrum of different aspects of war: the increasing complexity of war technology and motivations, the politics of war, war as a profession and so on.

Note that Thucydides's history was the first work of the kind in which events are traced to their *cause* and their *political lessons* brought out.

1.2 a) This note-taking activity allows students time to clarify and assimilate their first ideas and attitudes.
   b) – Of course Shannon's attitude is ironic, as the quotation for the unit clearly underlines. His approach to war is conditioned by his wish to find a job.
   – He would be unemployed in time of peace. So what is good for everyone else would be bad for him.
   – A 'good war' would presumably be well-paid, and with no CIA links (the American Central Intelligence Agency), therefore mercenaries would be free to fight for the power which paid best.

– Open response. Students should explain why they would or would not like such a job. A class debate might be organised on the subject.
– Open response.
c) Open response.
d) Two extremes in ways of presenting war in popular literature: humour and horror in comics. What other ways of presenting war can students think of? If copies are available, you could compare reporting on a war news event, for example, in the popular daily papers (*Sun, Daily Mirror, Daily Mail*) and in the 'heavies' (*Times, Guardian, Daily Telegraph*) (cf. Unit 7 Simulation). The *Asterix* extract distances events from reality in many ways. We laugh at the *characters* rather than the events. Students might find that the horror of war is enjoyable as presented in comics because one is not involved in it, and is never likely to be.

2.1 Text A William Shakespeare, *Henry V* 🔊

Henry is commanding, patriotic, persuasive. Shannon is obedient (but a free agent), cynical, matter-of-fact.
a) manhood: ll.3–17
   parenthood: ll.18–23
   patriotism: ll.25–28, 34
   pride: the whole speech
   nobility: ll.17–19, 29–30
b) Lines 6–17, 31–32.
c) 'imitate the action of the tiger' (l.6)
  'Let it pry through...the head, Like the brass cannon' (ll.10–11)
  'As fearfully as doth a gallèd rock' (l.12)
  'Fathers, that like so many Alexanders' (l.19)
  'stand like greyhounds in the slips' (l.31)
Mention at this point that a simile is a figure of speech in which one thing is likened to another. It is an *explicit* comparison (as opposed to the metaphor where the comparison is implicit) and uses such words as 'like' or 'as' ('like', 'imitate' in the lines above).
The King wants to incite the men to action with ideas of strength, energy, invincibility, speed – and the similes convey just these ideas. The similes are so forceful that the men are made to feel a sense of *identity* with 'the tiger', 'the brass cannon', the 'gallèd rock', their fathers, Alexander (the Great), and 'greyhounds'.

War

d) Line 15.
e) Henry would have distinguished between men (who could be noble) and beasts (who could not). The soldiers he is addressing would have made no such distinction; Henry is being inconsistent with his own convictions in order to convince his men.

2.2   a) You might like to show a picture of Shakespeare's theatre; Henry would have been surrounded by the audience on three sides, as if the speech were being made to *them*. They were probably moved by the speech.
   Acting out will underline the effectiveness of the direct address, and the rhetorical tricks that can be deployed: addressing different sections of the audience, pauses, changes of tone and emphasis, and so on. Do students think the audience is likely to be more affected by the sentiments of the speech or by the theatrical effect? Will its effect be different on a modern audience, compared to Shakespeare's own audience? Do students find the idea of the Shakespearean thrust stage more attractive, or less, than a more traditional proscenium stage?
   b) Open response.
   c) Open response.

3.1 Text B   Wilfred Owen, *Anthem for Doomed Youth*

Students should not answer the pre-question until 3.2(b). Owen's point of view is that of someone who is personally and physically involved in the war: he served as an infantry officer, was awarded a decoration for bravery, and was killed a week before the armistice. Students are likely to think it is written by an 'outsider' because of 'those who' in the first line and the third person plural throughout – it is Owen's way of distancing himself from the horror, a distancing he rejected in later poems. Get students to compare Owen's 'their'/'them' (notice there is no subject 'they') with Rosenberg's 'we' and Sassoon's 'I'.
   The questions on the poem are answered in pairs or groups, each answering one question only (7 pairs in a class of 14, 7 groups of 3 in a class of 21, for example). The activity is intended to create awareness of:
   – the contribution that single aspects make to the poem as a whole;

– the need to examine specific aspects or parts in the context of the whole.

a) 'passing-bells' (l.1) – the bells that sound for a funeral; 'the stuttering rifles' rapid rattle Can patter' (ll.3–4) – alliteration of t and r to sound like gunfire, leading to 'orisons' (l.4) – prayers for the dead. 'Prayers' or 'bells' (l.5) would be 'mockeries', the only 'choirs' are 'wailing shells' (l.7). Only line 8 brings us home, away from the battlefield, with the bugle call that will never be answered.

b) These emphasise the 'monstrous' presence of the war, denying all the usual rites ('passing-bells', 'orisons', 'prayers', 'bells', 'mourning') and replacing them with sounds of war.

c) At home (in Britain) – the counties where the dead soldiers came from, and where their families remain.

d) 'candles' (l.9), 'shine', 'glimmers' (l.11) – yellow; 'pallor' (l.12) – white, contrasting with 'pall' (l.12) – black. The last line closes out the light in house windows – light turns to darkness.

e) These are evocations of religion and church services, with undertones of purity and innocence in stark contrast with the experience of war. 'Shrill, demented' (l.7) are the exact opposite of the sounds that should be heard in this context, 'holy' (l.11) as it is, recalling choirboys (l.10) who should carry candles – instead the poet emphasises 'their eyes' (l.10), full of tears, religious ceremony overtaken by emotion.

f) The people in the 'sad shires' (l.8), the 'boys' (l.10) and 'girls' (l.12) who remember the dead.

g) The rhymes are largely monosyllabic and heavy, emphasising the sadness of the poem. 'Cattle (l.1) and 'rattle' (l.3) stand out rather shockingly, emphasising the vastness of the slaughter and the incessant repetition of the shooting. 'Guns' (l.2) / 'orisons' (l.4) and 'choirs' (l.6) / 'shires' (l.8) are rather unexpected rhymes, and all the more effective for being so. Rhyme scheme: a b a b c d c d e f f e g g.

3.2 a) Pairs or groups report on their findings. They will find that the answer to one question often helps to answer another, and that they have to agree on fundamental points of interpretation.

b) Students now answer the pre-question in the light of 3.2(a). The war is the First World War.

27

War

4.1 Text C Isaac Rosenberg, *Returning, We Hear the Larks*
Siegfried Sassoon, *Everyone Sang* 🔲

Students will notice the shared joy in birdsong. Rosenberg
describes more specific elements of horror, where Sassoon only
hints at prison and 'horror'. So the setting of the Sassoon poem
is less clear. The effect and impact are similar to those of the
Rosenberg which is, however, more clearly a 'war' poem.

4.2 Rosenberg's poem
a) The adjectives describing the pain of war – 'anguished',
'poison-blasted' – are firmly anchored to the physical
situation. The exceptions – 'strange', 'unseen', 'upturned
list'ning' (listening) – concentrate on what is beyond the
physical limits of the situation, and occur between the
description of the present situation from which the soldiers
are terrified they will never escape (the 'track' only 'opens on
our camp'), and the escape world of blindness and dreams.
b) No length is indicated. Discuss why we imagine the song
does not last long.
c) Only shades of dark and light are given, no colours as such:
'Sombre', 'the dark', 'blind', 'dark hair'. 'Upturned list'ning
faces' gives a lighter shade.
d) The joy which arrives so suddenly with the song – and its
converse, death, which could just as easily drop from the
sky, through cannon fire or bombs.

Sassoon's poem
e) The effect is of lifting, of lightness, which underlines the
uplift conveyed in the strong verbs like 'burst' and 'winging',
and confirms the emotional uplift the singing brings about.
f) It conveys the collective identity of the singers, and includes
'I' (the poet himself). The capital E is, in fact, used throughout the poem, but it is only its third occurrence, in mid-line,
which shows this.
g) The longer lines confirm the idea of the endlessness of the
singing, breaking out from the limited confines of the
preceding lines.

4.3 Open response. Students relate the aspects of war presented in
the texts to personal views, feelings and experiences.

5 Simulation 🔲

Recommended duration: Listening 5 minutes
(a) 10 minutes
(b)   5 minutes
(c) 15 minutes
(d) 30 minutes? (Duration depends on number of students.)

Students *listen* to the speech first (the delivery is part of it) and
read it afterwards.

You will almost certainly find that most students will wish to
argue *against* going to war. If none of your students are in
favour, they have only one choice at stage (d): to deliver the
arguments as speeches. If at all possible, avoid asking students
to present views which are not their own.

6 Simile and metaphor

a) The ideas and feelings expressed in the examples of simile
   and metaphor that the students collect cannot, of course, be
   expressed in any other way without changing them. What
   does this fact suggest, given that literature uses so much
   metaphor? Do all different expressions of an idea have
   different effects? Can students imagine Henry V's speech in
   Churchill's (largely non-metaphorical) style, and vice versa?

   Do not launch into a description of figurative devices; one
   effect of all these exercises will be to teach students that
   'literary' language can only in a very unsatisfactory way be
   analysed on the basis of 'figures of speech'.

   Students should be given definitions of simile and
   metaphor. A *simile* is a comparison of one thing with
   another, and uses a linguistic *sign* of comparison ('like',
   'as...as', etc.).

   A *metaphor* is a use of words to indicate something
   different from the literal meaning, and does *not* have a
   formal sign of comparison.

b) The cartoon makes fun of some traditional metaphorical
   associations. Aspiration is seen as distance; limits as the
   fence; the possible as the path; stability as the earth; love as
   flowers; the ephemeral as the ripples on a pond, death and
   decay as the felled tree (cf. Unit 2); lyricism as the singing
   bird; growth and change as the tree.

Elicit students' reactions to being surrounded (book in hand!) by such a welter of metaphors. Is the result that they lose their effectiveness as images? Can students find, or think of, other traditional, over-used metaphors?

c) Students should work in pairs or small groups on this activity.

There is only one simile: 'these who die as cattle'. The poem is crowded with metaphors. Associations of light and dark have already been noted (3.1(d) and (e)). Notice also 'pallor'/'pall' (l.12), the one denoting paleness, the other heavy darkness, which is then emphasised in the last line. The whole sextet builds on images of eyes and seeing or not seeing, to bring out more deeply the references to light and dark.

POSTSCRIPT

War is nothing more than the continuation of politics by other means.

Karl von Clausewitz, *On War*

4 Women

She could not have been 'a nice woman'.

This unit will bring out any feminist or male-chauvinist attitudes
in classes, so it might be as well, at the outset, to elicit feelings
on the subject, without going too deeply into the rights and
wrongs of it. The preliminary illustrations and quotations will
help you with this. The texts have been chosen to reflect
particularly strongly held or ingrained feelings, and so are more
deliberately provocative than those in most other units, as this
unit's quotation (from *Middlemarch*) confirms. The Patmore
text (1.1) is rather patronisingly Victorian, the McEwan text a
trick; the George Eliot passage shows how 'society' judges, the
Shakespeare and Boston Women's Collective texts are more
obviously 'feminist' in tone, but could hardly be further apart in
time.

As there is more danger here than usual of the discussion
getting out of hand, the activities attempt to channel it to
specific aspects and insist on close reference to the texts; it helps
to keep quite rigidly to them with more exuberant classes.

1.1 Theme

a) Open response.
b) Patmore was, in a particularly Victorian self-satisfied way,
being serious. What is more interesting is how students react
to the idea of 'difference' between men and women, how
seriously *they* take the notion. This will lead to a discussion
of difference.

Examples of 'fixed' ideas, etc., might be sexual roles,
domestic roles, marriage and career roles, parental roles
(father as parent, mother as wage-earner), single parent
families. Judgements are included in these, but there are also
the old ones: women as 'the weaker sex'; the phrase that the
wife must 'love, honour, *and obey*' her husband (italics ours)
in the wedding service; and many others, some of which will
doubtless emerge from students.

Consider how guilty we all are of some such divisive
thinking. Even to entitle a unit 'Women' (in a book written

31

by two men) might be considered a rather masculine approach!

c) The Doctor's attitude in the Chopin excerpt seems very close to Patmore's. There is an altogether different tone, however.

1.2 This allows the class (especially the women in it) to talk about men as well as women. *Attitudes* to the opposite sex are important in reading Text A.

2.1 Text A Ian McEwan, *Dead As They Come* 📼

This passage involves a trick, which the author plays in the story too; he does not reveal *what* the woman is until later in the story, thus building up reader expectations and reactions, only to reverse them. The secret is not revealed until 2.2 – it is vital that students work through with no suspicion of what the secret is.

a) Reaction to the passage will, at first, emphasise the male chauvinism of an arrogant, rich ('all my millions' (l.51)), selfish man ('I am a man in a hurry' (l.13)) who thinks he can 'buy' a woman. Women may react strongly to the idea of the woman as only beauty, clothes, posture, etc., which men may not have considered to be an objectionable viewpoint on women. Suggestions as to what the woman *might* do for a living will be limited – probably 'don't know', 'no evidence', prostitution, or modelling will be the only suggestions. Do not give the 'correct' answer yet.

Together the words give a picture of a very affected woman. Dictionary reference will bring out the artificiality of the woman and the rather old-fashioned pleasure the man derives from this very unnaturalness. 'Playful lapdogs' (l.7) and 'beckon' (l.14) seem to indicate a mature, oldish man, perhaps looking at a rather younger, very stylish, fastidious woman. Students may be influenced by the man's description to judge the woman harshly.

A lot of words, such as 'fools' (l.16), 'sexless, mincing' (l.20), 'execrable' (l.22), are value judgements on kinds of women which contrast with the woman being praised. 'Beyond' (l.25), 'disdained' (l.27), 'she understood, as only the great portrait painters of the eighteenth century understood' (ll.34–36) confirm that the man credits the woman with sharing his own attitudes, thus reinforcing his favour-

able judgement of her. Almost any phrase in the second paragraph can be considered in this context. 'Beauty is in the eye of the beholder'.
b) The lyricism is in the lines immediately before, especially the last sentence ('Her body ... sartorial artifice' (ll.37–41)) with its exaggerated vocabulary – 'tender counterpoint' (l.40), etc. The eulogy begins around 'It was autumn' (l.29). The language used is, in itself, attractive, even flattering (ask female students how they would feel if the words were addressed to them – flattered, mistrustful, embarrassed, foolish), while at the same time being bombastic, self-indulgent, exaggerated. More than convincing us of the seriousness of the man's feelings, it begins to arouse suspicion about his intentions. Do students think his lyricism promises well for how he would treat the woman?
c) Her 'beauty' (ll.25, 28), her superiority ('beyond' (l.25), 'disdained' (l.27)), her intelligence (cf. the comparison with 'great portrait painters' (ll.34–36)), 'her perfect body' (l.40), and the fact that she was 'another class of being' (l.23).
d) Open response. Points: How important are clothes? What is more important: looks, tidiness, elegance, etc., or something else? 'All that glisters is not gold'; 'You can't judge a book by the cover'; 'Beauty is only skin deep'. Is ugliness the opposite of beauty?
e) This implies the sensuousness, the range of attractive uses to which rich materials (silk, velvet, etc.) can be put, evoking the sense of sight as well as touch, making us think, perhaps, of rich folds, deep colours and textures, as well as the purity of white fabric, the 'nuance' of simplicity. Are students sensitive to fabric? (Women more than men?)
f) She seems to have a lot of clothes – a range for each season, sometimes changing every day. Perhaps she is very rich; the words 'disdained' and 'discarded' (l.27) indicate a carelessness which might confirm this. Students might get the idea here that she is a fashion model, but don't encourage them too much if not.
g) This rather revealing exclamation shows something more human about the man – a kind of boyish nervousness at the thought of first real contact with the woman he loves. It might make the man a little more attractive than he has been up to now. Men might identify a little more closely with him. The feeling is a common one, but 'the approach' question shows something of social habits which should cause reaction. Why can't (or shouldn't) a woman ask a man to dance, for example? Are things changing in this respect?

2.2 Checking on the answers already given (if notes have been kept, or the blackboard used to keep points in mind, so much the better) quick character studies should emerge, perhaps slightly more detailed than the first impressions (see 2.1(a)) but not radically different. Don't spend too much time on it, but allow students to formulate their attitudes to and opinions of the man and woman. These will almost certainly be negative, and the stronger the better, because they will change when you reveal the 'secret' – the woman is a plastic model dummy in a fashion shop window. Students should now re-read the passage: what was not clear will become so; everything should fall into place. The reaction might be laughter, pity (for the man), even irritation – all judgements will have to be reconsidered, that is the important point.

3.1 **Text B** George Eliot, *Middlemarch* 📼

George Eliot certainly does not share in the general judgement of Dorothea – this is the main point of the passage. Rather she wants to show how false and meaningless it is to judge as 'not... "a nice woman"' (l.35) (the inverted commas show something of the author's attitude) one who 'married a sickly clergyman' (ll.30–31) and then 'his cousin' (l.32). Point out that George Eliot was the pseudonym of Mary Ann Evans – a woman.

a) First, Dorothea's own impression of herself is unambitious, with the reserve that things might have been 'better' (l.2) 'if she had only been better and known better' (ll.3–4). This implies a negative judgement on some aspect(s) of her past. Her marriage is, however, positive in her own eyes, with 'love' (l.7), 'emotion' (l.10) and 'activity' (l.11). The author, towards the end of the first paragraph, seems to sympathise with Dorothea, while reporting the opinions of 'Many who knew her' (ll.19–20) and who had considered her positively ('so substantive and rare a creature' (ll.20–21)).

Sir James's view of the marriage is decidedly 'negative' (l.25). (Do students feel this implies a basically positive idea towards Dorothea? In fact, Sir James was an early suitor to Dorothea and, being rejected, married her younger sister.)

In Middlemarch Dorothea was considered 'a fine girl' (l.30). So it is generally her second marriage which causes negative comment. George Eliot presents both sides of the argument in the third and fourth paragraphs, contrasting what was 'not ideally beautiful' (ll.37–38) with the 'not widely visible' (l.52) 'fine issues' (l.51). It is this that gives us

the clue to George Eliot's sympathies: no one is perfect , and
all of us can be judged, but her own sympathy emerges from
the last paragraph as strongly for Dorothea.

   'Theresa' (l.43) is Saint Theresa, a sixteenth century Spanish
saint who, in the words of Eliot's prelude to *Middlemarch*,
'found her epos in the reform of a religious order'. 'Antigone'
(l.45) is the character in Sophocles's play who defies law and
society to bury her brother. 'Cyrus' (l.53) is the founder of
the Persian empire.

b) Her two marriages.

c) The regret hinted at is not expanded upon. 'Still' (l.4)
    introduces the compensations for any such regret – the
    marriage to Will, and his growing career, and their family.
    Others think 'it a pity' (l.20) that she did not achieve more,
    echoing her own regret, but without voicing any compen-
    sation or any alternative.

d) The words 'what else ... she ought rather to have done'
    (ll.23–24) seem to indicate that the author, in observing the
    lack of constructive possibilities in the 'Many who knew her'
    (ll.19–20), is being ironic about their superiority, their
    ability to judge but not to help.

e) 'She had now a life filled also with a beneficent activity
    *which she had not the doubtful pains of discovering and
    marking out for herself*' (ll.10–12), and 'she should give him
    wifely help' (l.19). This is linked to the last paragraph by its
    mention of unseen assistance and contributions to the
    'reforms' (l.13) and the righting of 'wrongs' (l.17) which,
    from that day ('those times' (l.13)) to this ('our days' (l.15)),
    have helped 'the growing good of the world' (ll.55–56) and
    helped things to be 'not so ill with you and me as they might
    have been' (ll.57–58).

f) The difference lies in the contexts in which the words are
    applied. Will can be 'ardent' and committed in his public
    work, helping the 'beneficent activity' (ll.10–11) of the
    period; his personal crusade is for the public good. The
    'ardent deeds' of Saint Theresa and Antigone are symbolic
    actions expressive of a world that no longer exists: the
    actions may still have some symbolic significance, but the
    ardour which instigated and inspired them is not relevant to
    the modern world. The 'ardent' of line 12, therefore, implies
    what in our own times has come to be called 'committed'.

g) George Eliot is evaluating both Dorothea and the falsity of
    society's judgements. The final effect is one of acceptance of
    the inevitability and pity of situations like Dorothea's:
    freedom and fulfilment are relative concepts, and each of us

must find his or her own level of satisfaction. Gray's *Elegy Written in a Country Churchyard* (Unit 9) would be a useful cross-reference.

h) This does not presume a knowledge of the period. Rather it draws on students' sensitivity to present-day conditions in relation to what emerges from the passage. For example, the reaction to Dorothea's second marriage would certainly not be so strong nowadays. Women's freedom of choice would therefore seem to have become much less limited, Dorothea's individuality being an exception to the general rule at the time the author was writing.

3.2 Open response.

4.1 Text C William Shakespeare, *Othello* 📼

'They' are men; 'we' and 'us' are women.

a) Giving insufficient attention to their wives (sexually) and giving what is due to their wives to others (ll.2–3) ('foreign' means here only 'alien'; 'our' therefore means 'which should be ours'); reacting in petty jealous ways restricting the wives' freedom (ll.4–5); using physical violence (l.5); or reducing our allowances to spite us (l.6). (This has also been interpreted as 'speaking belittlingly of what we used to be' (before marriage); the sense of the phrase is clearer without too close an analysis.)

b) The affirmations of what men *might* do are now questioned for motivation, and each question is so phrased that it leads to a positive answer, as seen from the female point of view.

c) Open response. Is she being over-divisive, making a 'them' and 'us' situation, or is she right to do so?

d) It confirms it. The reasoning of the three questions and answers (ll.11–15) and the further three questions left unanswered (although the answers are clearly 'Yes' to all three) (ll.15–16) have taken the case to its logical conclusion.

e) Open response. Emilia stresses similarity, Patmore difference.

f) Open response.

4.2 Emilia's speech is more immediate, being a speech, and being a well-constructed, almost debate-like piece of reasoning. George Eliot has more time to let us know something of Dorothea, and to present a less clear-cut analysis of a question, which is not so easily resolvable as that posed by Emilia. George Eliot, there-fore, has more of a balance of sympathy and objectivity. The fact that we speak of George Eliot and of Emilia (not of Shakespeare) shows the forcefulness of Emilia's words – this might be seen by some as a weakness in her case.

5 Text D Boston Women's Health Collective, *Our Bodies Ourselves* [cassette icon]

a) It is modern, factual, uncompromising, committed, almost scientific in its approach. It is not until 'We' in the second sentence of the second paragraph that it becomes clear that it was written by women (for women). The commitment becomes progressively clearer.

b) The mention of '"having" to be a housewife' (l.9) might echo part of Dorothea's problem. Talk of 'outlets' (l.10) recalls Emilia's words. Human relationships seen as 'power relationships' might recall the first impressions of the man and woman in *Dead As They Come*, notably in 'Women are in comparison relatively powerless' (ll.38–39).

c) It should be abundantly clear from its tone and content that the passage is fully in sympathy with women's plight, and was written by women to show other women that they were not alone in their problems, and perhaps also to make men aware of some of these problems.

d) The injustices are the restrictions, frustrations, and limi-tations either actively or passively imposed on women – the inability to react, turning 'feelings inwards' (l.27), the fact that 'we cannot easily leave home' (l.35), financial depen-dence of women 'totally reliant on their husbands' incomes' (ll.56–57), homefinding difficulties, children, battering, etc. It may be useful to refer to Unit 5, Authority.

e) Open response. Some men think that women are complain-ing unjustifiably, that the problems are not widespread. Is this opinion shared? Do men have similar grievances against women?

6 Simulation

It is important that students read the extracts *after* studying their roles.

PROCEDURE

i) Division into groups of 6 and assignment of roles (5 minutes).
ii) Students study their roles (10 minutes).
iii) Students (in their roles) read the extracts (15 minutes).
iv) Discussion of reactions (10 minutes).
v) Students write letters (20 minutes).
vi) Students playing the same roles (all the Dorotheas, for example) compare their letters (10 minutes).

Total duration: 70 minutes.

7 Sexist language

a) This is designed to make students think of the unconscious ways in which sex roles are handled in language terms. 'Sexist' can be applied to any language use which implies a judgement of superiority (usually male). Reference might be made to almost any unit. For example, notice in Rebellion (p.70) how few women there are, confirmed in the Postscript; in Ideals notice Coleridge's word 'damsel' (pp.83–84) – elicit other words which describe and categorise: maid, lady, spinster, harridan, tart, slut, etc. Notice how few have male equivalents, and how many imply a judgement (usually unfavourable to women). In Family (p.1) notice how strongly women are placed in traditional roles, stressing the *assumption* that these roles are proper and normal. The few cases which give predominance to women do not balance out the overall predominance of male voices and attitudes. Is this because literature has reflected the respective roles of men and women (or is it because *Reading between the lines* was written by two men)? Students might be directed to Virginia Woolf's *A Room of One's Own* for extended reading on the subject.

b) The jokiness of 'herstory', etc., is a reflection of a growing awareness, notably on the part of women, of their voice and role in society. (Cf. Angela Carter, 'The Language of Sisterhood', and Randolph Quirk, 'Sound Barriers and *Gangbangspreche*' in *The State of the Language*, ed. L.Michaels and C.Ricks, California University Press, 1980, and *Words and Women* by C.Miller and K.Swift, Penguin, 1977.) The syndrome is reflected in the language of minorities (blacks, gays, etc.) – but are women to be considered a minority? Elicit reactions to this, to feminism, traditional and modern roles, expressions in the students' mother-tongue, etc. ('mother-tongue' is an example of sexist classification too; and 'fatherland'?). The question might result in written work expressing students' reflections on the whole subject. S/he has been proposed as an alternative to he/she – but it leaves the problem of his/her unsolved.

c) The areas which are largely feminine in linguistic orientation are child care, cooking (but not *haute cuisine*), and love (in its romantic connotations), all emphasising the traditional domestic role of women. Cars and ships are often called 'she' – perhaps by extension a reference to male possession? Teachers of certain subjects or age-groups are often expected (by pupils) to be male (especially for scientific subjects) while female teachers might be preferred for 'more artistic' subjects. Elicit students' preferences and expectations and ask them to justify them. The Angela Carter quotation might also apply to the students' own language. Again, it might be used as a title for written work.

d) Open response. How many students really believe that men and women are *completely* equal?

POSTSCRIPT

What vain unnecessary things are men.
How well we do without 'em.

John Wilmot, Earl of Rochester, *Draft of a Satire on Man*

5 Authority

That is how we tell whether or not we live in a free country.

This unit presents *attitudes* to authority as well as aspects of the topic, and the Theme section is designed to reveal students' attitudes. The passages are often humorous, although the authority they show is usually rather frightening – this ambivalence is vital to all the discussions that will arise. Keep referring to how students would feel in each situation described and elicit how they would react; these attempts at identification with the characters build up to the simulation.

1   Theme

a) Students concentrate on observable detail to open up the topic and bring useful ideas and vocabulary to the fore. In the photograph of Mussolini, students will pick on details like the uniform (boots, belt, etc.), the Latin motto, Mussolini's stance and facial expression, the attendant officer, and the footstool setting the 'Duce' above everyone else.

  Some relevant characteristics of the language of the Ten Commandments are:
  – the emphatic imperative, using the subject
  – the strong negative 'shalt have no' / 'shalt not'
  – the numbered list
  – the antiquated forms
  – the use of capitals for LORD

b) Open response. Students work in groups to investigate the attitudes that personal experience has formed in them. The questions put the parent in the role of 'a higher official' (see the Steiner quotation accompanying the illustrations) and try to elicit some of the taboos of parental authority. The anecdotes that the questions elicit will often be humorous.

2.1 Text A   Lewis Carroll, *Alice in Wonderland* 📼

Students read silently; reserve the recording till later(2.3).

The Hatter has, of course, done nothing wrong, except to
irritate the King and Queen.
a) Because he is afraid of the court, and the power of the King
and Queen.
b) As far as we know, they said nothing.
c) Because they cheered.
d) Open response. Suggested vocabulary: imperious, tyrannical,
dictatorial, etc.
e) Probably not.
f) Probably not; they just enjoy exercising their authority.

2.2 a) Some examples are:
– 'I deny it!' said the March Hare.
'He denies it,' said the King: 'leave out that part.'
... and the following sentence, with its insistence on
'deny'/'denied' (lines 43–44).
– 'I'm a poor man, your Majesty,' he began.
'You're a *very* poor *speaker*,' said the King. (ll. 52–54)
– The play on 'suppressed' in lines 56–68.
– The play on 'stand down' / 'go no lower' / 'sit down' in
lines 64–67.
b) Lines 31–34 are an example. The effect is to negate all
relationship between the King and his subjects and to stress
the impression of unjustified power.

2.3 Following students' first attempt at a reading, play the recording. They might like to try again. Draw attention to the limited
range of communicative functions the King uses and which
express his authority: *insistence* ('Of course twinkling begins
with a T!'), *order* ('Go on!'), *threat* ('or I'll have you executed'),
granting permission ('You may stand down').

2.4 Open response. (a) and (b) relate back to 1 (Mussolini and the
Ten Commandments), and (c) draws on what has been gained
from reading the Lewis Carroll passage.
Try to elicit specific examples of language use. They *do* differ
greatly, of course, from individual to individual: teachers tend
to use a great many imperatives, while entertainers ensure
attention by making what they say interesting, humorous.
Students may like to speculate on the effect of teachers changing
their role of maintaining their authority to that of entertainer,
for example.

3.1 Text B George Orwell, *Nineteen Eighty-Four* 📼

a) The Thought Police are people employed by the State to look into everyone's thoughts, words and actions.

b) Big Brother is the symbol of State Control of everything, constantly watching every individual.

c) It makes him live constantly with the idea that everything he does is watched – we imagine, therefore, that he is very careful in everything he says, does, or even thinks.

d) For example: 'every commanding corner' (l.7), 'the dark eyes looked deep into Winston's own' (l.9), 'like a blue-bottle' (l.13), and all of the last paragraph!

e) He feels the police patrol is an intrusion into people's privacy, and that the telescreen's talk is meaningless. This shows both a distrust of and a lack of respect for authority.

f) Open response.

3.2 Open response. It is important that students note Orwell's use of realistic touches in his description of a kind of horror fantasy that often seems to be becoming more and more real.

4 Text C Joseph Heller, *Catch-22* 📼

The order is (Group Headquarters), Colonel Cathcart, (Major Danby), Doc Daneeka, ex-P.F.C. (Pilot First Class) Wintergreen, Yossarian, Hungry Joe.

a) Fifty-five.

b) Yossarian wants to go home. But Colonel Cathcart wants him to fly more missions. Twenty-seventh Air Force Headquarters allows a pilot to go home after forty missions. But Colonel Cathcart has to be obeyed. So Yossarian has to fly fifty-five missions.

c) Catch-22 is that you have to obey your commanding officer even if he is wrong or goes against regulations. Notice the emphatic use of 'do' in line 28.

d) Lines 1 to 9 show a kind of enthusiastic madness and self-esteem which take no account of the men. This may be considered rather frightening, although Heller's lightness of tone makes it seem funny, if chilling.

e) Big Brother's authority is gloomily all-pervasive and brooks no discussion. Apart from the fact that Colonel Cathcart has the touch of madness noted in (d), and the possibility which Yossarian has of flying to and fro to discuss things, Colonel

Cathcart's authority is much the same, although he has a superior (27th Air Force HQ) to whom he is answerable while Big Brother is all powerful.

f) Three times. It adds emphasis to the tension of Yossarian's predicament, and gives an unusual 'break' to what *seems* to be largely dialogue.

g) With the line 'We'd probably shoot you' (l.43) ex-P.F.C. Wintergreen shows that he has switched loyalties. He is no longer on Yossarian's side, as he might have seemed when Yossarian first 'flew to visit' him (l.8). His 'we' puts him on Colonel Cathcart's side. This is a good example of how authority claims loyalty against logic, reason, or comradeship; ex-P.F.C. Wintergreen wants to keep himself in the right. It is the resultant loneliness of his position which brings home to Yossarian the strength of Colonel Cathcart's authority.

h) Students might note 'infused with the democratic spirit' (l.2), lines 3 and 4, 5 and 6, 19 and 20, and so on. Notice that Heller's humour comes from building up expectations (fifty missions – then fifty-five, etc.) and exploding them – but always with a truthfulness such as we see in ex-P.F.C. Wintergreen's last reply.

i) It is meaningful and appropriate in this context because of the element of challenge, and it well expresses Yossarian's frustration at being placed in a situation where he is helpless to react.

5 Text D Joe Orton, *Loot*

Wait until students have answered questions (a) to (e) before explaining. Truscott is a police inspector. In order not to arouse suspicion he is pretending to be from the Water Board. A bank has been robbed. Hal always tells the truth (so he *did* help to rob the bank). The scene is in Hal's home. The money is in his dead mother's coffin (her body is in a wardrobe in the room where the action is taking place). It is being buried – her funeral is taking place simultaneously. Fay is the nurse who looked after Hal's mother. See answer (e).

a) Yes – the interrogation becomes real, and frightening.

b) His authority is being frustrated (by the truth, what's more!). He reacts against 'cheek', against 'kids' who 'treat any kind of authority as a challenge'. Do students agree with him?

c) The humour is based on wordplay and contrast – 'He's only a boy' is a common phrase which Truscott takes literally, 'I'm not impressed by his sex.' Truscott's treatment of Hal is in humorous (black humour) contrast with his words – 'that is how we tell whether or not we live in a free country' and 'Under any other political system I'd have you on the floor in tears'.

d) Hal is guilty, the Hatter was not. So Hal has more reason to be nervous. His situation in the face of authority is similarly worrying. Truscott's investigation has a logical illogicality which recalls the King and Queen.

e) See introduction above. The priest is not an accomplice, but the funeral director is. Hal could find no other place to hide the money.

6 Simulation

Recommended duration: Preliminary tasks 20+ minutes
Simulation   45 minutes

This is a whole-class simulation with nine principal roles and the rest of the class playing members of a jury. You may be tempted, if your class is large (25 or more), to have two groups perform the simulation simultaneously; you would do well to refrain from this unless two rooms are available since the activity is complicated and gives rise to heated discussion.

Since the preparation to be carried out, including that of the jury members, is substantial, it is useful to set it for homework.

7 Style

Work has been done on the individual passages of the unit which will enable students to attempt characterisations of the type requested. Get them to refer to answers to / notes on 1(a), 2.2(a) and (b), and 5(c).

Be satisfied if the students' attention is drawn to the idea of style, and don't be too concerned with their ability to express the differences.

POSTSCRIPT

A dog's obeyed in office.

William Shakespeare, *King Lear*

6 Indifference

I am – yet what I am none cares or knows.

It is more usual in classrooms to bring to the surface positive reactions and attitudes, rather than a negative one like indifference. And yet indifference, not caring, is notable at any time and, some would say, particularly in our modern world. Awareness of indifference is seen in the many advertisements for help for the aged, appeals for voluntary work, attempts to involve the public in conservation, etc. Someone once said, 'I am more hurt by someone's indifference towards me than by any other emotion.'

1 Theme

Open response. The juxtaposition of the posters should provoke some reaction other than indifference! Points which might be brought out: contrast between Western concerns with beauty, elegance, fashion, etc. and more basic Eastern or Third World concerns of famine, illness, poverty. Who cares?

2.1 Text A Emily Dickinson, *Nobody* 📼

a) The use of dashes is typical of Emily Dickinson. Commas are unusual in her work. Capital letters ('Nobody – Too' (l.2)) are common. Both give a kind of breathless emphasis to the words: she uses very few words but each and every one is very important to the whole poem, and the most important words are given further emphasis through dashes and capital letters. Notice the difference in effectiveness if the poem is read straight through (without particular emphasis) and if it is read observing dashes and stressing capital-letter words. Notice the tentative questioning tone of the second line and the 'dreariness' of the fifth.

b) To keep the secret of the two nobodys to themselves. The gesture of index finger to the lips would emphasise the collaboration of secrecy.

c) 'They' are other people, the rest of the world. They'd

advertise, or broadcast the secret of the two nobodys because they'd want everyone to be the same, to be someone. It is not easy to be so different!   .

d) Its croaking. Notice the great deflating effect of the anti-climatic monosyllable 'Bog' – clearly an image of the world that would 'advertise'.

2.2   Open response.

3.1   Text B   John Clare, *I am* 🔲

Students might pick out: 'My friends forsake me like a memory lost' (l.2), 'death's oblivion lost' (l.5), 'the vast shipwreck of my life's esteems' (l.10). Instead of suffering the indifference of mankind, Clare would prefer 'scenes where man has never trod' (l.13) – a kind of Garden of Eden.

a) Some might find the first verse positive, but most probably will see nothing very positive until the peace and tranquillity of the third verse, around line 16.

b) The answer will probably be no – aloneness emerges more than comfort as the main theme of the poem.

c) Friends (l.2), sense of life, joys (l.9), life's esteems (l.10) – the things that contribute to making life worthwhile. They seem to have lost their importance to him because he has lost interest in people. Discussion point: is it the poet who has lost interest in others, or vice versa? Is this in any way symptomatic?

d) Basically he wants to escape from the problems and pressures of the world and other people and to find the innocence and peace he knew in childhood. The return to childhood theme is quite a common one. Students may well have or have had similar wishes, and this can lead to a discussion of reactions to the second part of the question.

e) The chaos in a dream-like world of oblivion where the poet's mind is troubled by his imaginings of being scorned, of noise, of uncomfortable visions and dreams, against the tide of which he must try to swim. (See also 3.2.)

f) Because they have been closer to you and you have under-stood them better (as you thought). Distance is therefore the more unexpected and seems inexplicable.

g) Esteems are the opinions other people hold of you, so they may be part of ideals and ambitions.

h) Open response.

3.2 a) 'The vast shipwreck of my life's esteems' (l.10).

b) Points: the confusion, the chaos, and the tide against which the poet swims (see answer 3.1(e)) lead to shipwreck – the destruction of all he held dear. The first metaphor is thus extended, elaborated and concluded.

c) 'like a memory lost' (l.2); 'like shades' (spirits of the dead) (l.5).

d) The similes and metaphors add a kind of evanescence to the things Clare is trying to grasp, strengthening the ideas of loss and abandonment in the poem. (Refer back to 3.1(h).)

3.3 Open response. 'S' recalls the sea, spirits, the whistling of air passing through emptiness.

4.1 Text C Christopher Isherwood, *Down There on a Visit*

Reactions are: satisfied (the other customer); toxic (the narrator); ostrich-like (the newsreel); playful (Dr Fisch).

a) In the barber's shop by describing conversation and reactions; in the cinema by contrasting the importance of the crisis in his own mind with the blandness and insecure happiness of the newsreel and by stressing the sadness of the man behind him; at Aunt Edith's by continual reference to the clock and the timing of the speech; at Dr Fisch's by actually discussing the crisis from another point of view.

b) – trying to make her shiver with fright
– my orientation in regard to where I am and what time it is
– as if blind to reality, burying one's head in the sand
– so fragile and uncertain to continue that it touched one's emotions
– helpful and giving useful support to
– a kind of teasing by pointing up a weak spot

c) Hitler each time.

d) Open response.

4.2 Open response. Some students might feel that indifference is a necessary shutting-off of emotional involvement, and that the media make us aware of far too many things that would be emotionally involving without the 'indifference mechanism'.

5.1 Text D W.H. Auden, *Musée des Beaux Arts* 🔊

   a) The Old Masters, who understood suffering, and never forgot its place in the great scheme of things.
   b) Lines 8 and 9, 13 and 14, 18 ('the sun shone'), and line 22.
   c) It might be death (rebirth into a new life).
   d) The ploughman, the sun shining, the white legs disappearing into the green ocean, the expensive delicate ship.
   e) Because everyone is indifferent to Icarus's tragedy. Life goes on.
   f) Open response (probably nothing!).

5.2 dreadful martyrdom / Anyhow ... untidy spot; torturer's horse / innocent behind; leisurely / disaster; something amazing / calmly.
These present the contrast between involved reaction and indifference.

6.1 Text E Dylan Thomas, *A Refusal to Mourn the Death, by Fire, of a Child in London* 🔊

   a) 'Never until X shall I ...' = I shall never (do something) until (something happens).
   b) Darkness. It tells (announces, as in 'to tell the time') 'the last light breaking' (the last dawn on earth).
   c) mankind making
   Bird beast and flower Fathering
   all humbling
   These composite adjectives show that man is made (conceived) in darkness, that darkness is the father of all nature, and everything and everyone is eventually reduced again to darkness.
   d) It will be made completely still.
   e) He will enter the Kingdom of Heaven. (A drop of water and an ear of corn are symbolic images of God's greatness – bread and water are the staff of life; the synagogue, a Jewish temple, continues the idea of Zion. The references are to the Old Testament of the Bible.) In short, he must die.
   f) To cry (tears are slightly salty). This continues the image of the 'water bead' in line 8.
   g) Murder; a grave truth; blaspheme.

h) Grave = tomb, or grave = serious; stations = stations of the cross, or stations = stopping points of breath, sobs.

i) The first people ever to have died; the death of the first person ever to have died. In short, all deaths are equal; it is just as useless to mourn this death as it would be to mourn the long-forgotten nameless dead of countless centuries ago. Discussion: is this a cynical, or necessary outlook? See also question 6.2.

j) They might be death's robes, or even the girl's coffin; but the implication also covers the memories of friends, and, by extension, the long friendship and community, the oneness of all mankind.

k) The River Thames.

l) He is affected by the death (otherwise he would not have written the poem!), awed by it; the poem however justifies his necessary refusal to mourn.

m) Not until the end of time, or of the world as we know it. Because death has to be accepted as a simple fact in this world (l.24).

6.2   Open response (see also answer 6.1(i)).

7 Simulation

Recommended duration: Stage (a)   10 minutes
(b)   10 minutes
(c)   30 minutes
Total 50 minutes

Students will naturally wish to be on the side of those who care, hence the invitation to identify with a local character. Letters are individual and can be written at home. The whole-class discussion is at stage (b).

8 The language of indifference and the language of caring

a) Students can range over a wide variety of language. They will discover, however, that language expressing indifference is rare: literature is written by people who care.

b) Open response.

POSTSCRIPT

The worst sin towards our fellow creatures is not to hate them, but to be indifferent to them; that's the essence of inhumanity.

G.B. Shaw, *The Devil's Disciple*

7 Rebellion

The be-all and end-all

This unit brings together texts which might seem to have nothing in common at first sight – *Animal Farm, Paradise Lost, Macbeth* and Iris Murdoch's *The Sacred and Profane Love Machine*. They are united by the theme of rebellion, and many complementary aspects will be found.

Following *Animal Farm*, the extract from *Paradise Lost* is meant to appear (and *be*) difficult. In reading literature, students must be prepared to face difficulties of many kinds, and to acquire the means to tackle them. The whole of *Reading between the lines* offers ample opportunities to do this, while the exercises accompanying the Milton passage direct attention at features causing specific problems. Do not, therefore, be daunted by this and the extract from *Macbeth* which follows it; there are good reasons for their inclusion.

1.1 Theme

a) Elicit examples of violence today (Ulster, Lebanon, race riots, etc.), without going into motivations too deeply. Is violence a useful or justifiable way to achieve one's aims? Is it ever successful?
b) Movement, crowds, facial expressions, etc.
c) Reaction and recounting. If this is outside students' direct experience, have them talk about news broadcasts they have heard/seen.
d) Some countries were created out of violence (Kenya, Cyprus, Algeria, Italy), others destroyed (who remembers Bosnia-Herzegovina, Serbia, Aden, Biafra, the Austro-Hungarian Empire?). Is terrorism in any form justifiable in our own times?

1.2 Dictionary work. Are 'rebellion' and 'uprising' the same? Bring out the distinction between the general application of 'rebellion' and the particular, when it does mean the same as 'uprising'.

2.1 **Text A** George Orwell, *Animal Farm* 🔊

a) Because they had not been fed, and then when they 'began to help themselves' (ll.27–28) they were attacked. Obviously they had been discontented with Mr Jones's regime for some time.

b) Mr Jones 'had become much disheartened' (ll.5–6) and taken to drink, leaving his farm to neglect. 'His men' (l.11) had consequently become 'idle and dishonest' (l.12) and the whole thing was going to the bad.

c) He is probably some kind of pet (see l.11). Only this can be deduced or imagined from the present extract. In fact, he is a tame raven, Mr Jones's special pet, much disliked by the animals.

d) The first sentence makes it clear that the animals' plans were not specific in terms of what would be done, or when. Then 'though nothing of the kind had been planned beforehand' (ll.33–34) confirms this at the moment when the revolt proper begins. 'At last they could stand it no longer' (ll.25–26) begins to set the Rebellion in motion. The men 'in the store-shed with whips in their hands, lashing out in all directions' (ll.30–31) drive the animals to violence, through their own violence.

e) A very short time: 'After only a moment' (ll.41–42) leads to 'A minute later' (l.43), and the animals have triumphed.

f) On the evening of Sunday 22nd June. The animals could have been fed either on the Friday, or on the Saturday morning.

g) Open response.

2.2 Encourage use of 'might have' or 'would have' forms. In fact, they explored the whole farm and eliminated all traces of humanity from it, and all 'anti-animal' equipment, then ate 'a double ration' of corn before settling down for the night.

2.3 This exercise will bring out similarities in expression and theme between Text A and Text B.

a) broke in (l.26), whips (l.30), lashing out (l.31), flung (l.34), butted and kicked (l.36), uprising (l.39), thrashing and maltreating (l.40), in full flight (l.44), pursuing (l.46).

b) He is recounting 'A Fairy Story', as he tells us in his sub-title to the book. Like an allegory, the simplicity of the animals' story hides (not very deeply) a serious moral concern in the fable.

c) The language used should clearly be seen to be modern. *Animal Farm* was first published in 1945.

3.1 Text B John Milton, *Paradise Lost* 🔲

Because of the nature of the exercise – learning how to work things out for yourself – *refrain from giving background information* about Milton, the subject of *Paradise Lost* (Satan and his followers were expelled by God from Heaven for disobedience), and the battle in this extract (between the powers of Heaven and Hell).

a) i) and ii) Play the recording of lines 32 to 44, or read them aloud, as they echo Orwell's battle, with 'storming fury rose' (l.32), 'clamour' (l.33), 'clashing brayed Horrible discord' (ll.34–35), 'raged' (l.36), 'dire was the noise Of conflict' (ll.36–37), 'dismal hiss' (l.37), all indicating sounds. Other violent words include 'madding' (l.35), 'flaming volleys' (l.38), 'fire' (l.39), 'rushed' (l.40), 'battles' (l.41), 'ruinous assault' (l.41), 'inextinguishable rage' (l.42). Compare these with the words picked out in question 2.3(a). Orwell's are words of action and movement, Milton's more of sound and movement – the effect is remarkably similar.

b) i) This question enables students to identify the participants and the parts they play.
– 'he' (l.14) raised his weapon and served Satan a blow on the head.
– Satan (l.16) took ten paces back and was forced to kneel.
– 'The rebel thrones' (l.24) were amazed and angry. They did nothing immediately.
– Michaël (l.27) sounded the trumpet to announce battle.
– 'the faithful armies' (l.29) praised God.
– 'The adverse legions' (l.31) joined in the battle.

ii) Answers are given in 3.1(c) of the Student's Book.

d) i) One of God's men, Abdiel in fact, is speaking to Satan, as can be seen from his insistence on 'God' (ll.1–9), on obedience and 'servitude' (l.3), and from the constant use of 'thee'/'thy'/'thine' (ll.5–6,

8, 12–13) contrasting with 'our' (l.7) and 'me' (ll.8,12). See also question 3.2(d).

ii) Dictionary work in preparation for questions (iii) to (vi).

iii) That the one who rules is the best fitted to do so, and is superior to those he rules. God's worthiness (ll.2,5) contrasts with 'the unwise' Satan.

iv) Servitude for Abdiel would be the opposite of his present position, as it would mean serving 'the unwise' (l.4), someone who is not worthy to be master, perhaps because he has rebelled against his master as Satan did. Those who serve Satan are thus in servitude (l.3) because Satan himself is not free to be the just and true master – 'Thy self not free' (l.6); rather he is imprisoned by the crime of his rebellion. Abdiel considers himself 'blest' (l.9) and happy in the service of God, who is 'worthiest to be obeyed' (l.10, echoing l.2). We can imagine that he would prefer to serve in Heaven than reign in Hell.

v) 'Thine' are Satan's followers, 'thee' is Satan himself. The third person pronouns refer to different characters: 'he' (ll.2–3) is used in general, meaning 'anyone who' (although the reference is indirectly to God; 'him'/'his' (ll.4–5) are similarly general ('anyone who hath rebelled') referring, by implication, to Satan; 'his' (l.9) refers directly to 'God' in the same line.

vi) Line 11 tells them to expect imprisonment ('chains') rather than blissful freedom ('realms').

e) 11–13: You should expect chains, not realms, in Hell; meanwhile, take on your head this greeting from me, now that I have, as you have just said, returned from my flight.

18–19: He recoiled (and retreated) ten huge paces.

32–34: Now storming fury and clamour, such as had never been heard in Heaven till now, rose.

Milton's word order gives greater stress to certain words – for example 'rose' (l.32), which loses all its impact when placed at the end of its sentence.

3.2 a) Orwell by words indicating action, Milton by words indicating sound and movement.

b) Milton was endeavouring to create an epic language

worthy of his subject – hence the 'poetic' style and use of language (greatly dependent on sound, as we have noticed) which came to be called Miltonic. Orwell's subject matter is equally serious, but his use of animals as characters (see question 2.3(b)) led him to use the deliberately simple language of the fable or fairy tale.

c) and d) Open response. The question gets students to focus on the *sense* of period. *Paradise Lost* was first published in 1667. Its language is clearly antiquated. Its style is peculiar to Milton, and the religious context (Old Testament) gives it a kind of religious resonance of tone.

e) Open response. Students have worked out much of the content of the *Paradise Lost* passage for themselves, with the guidance of the exercises. Point out that Milton himself gave his readers guidance in the 'Argument' (summary) prefacing each of the 12 books of *Paradise Lost*.

4.1 Text C William Shakespeare, *Macbeth*

a) The rhythms and pauses suggest Macbeth's agitation – he is confused.

b) The only positive possibility he sees is, if it were over quickly and success were immediate, avoiding 'the life to come' (l.7). All the rest is negative: 'judgement' (l.8), 'justice' (l.10), 'trust' (l.12), etc. The killing will not be over quickly – the consequences will always remain. Macbeth is Duncan's 'kinsman and his subject' (l.13), 'his host' (l.14), and Duncan has been a 'meek' (l.17), 'clear' (l.18) and virtuous king. Macbeth's motive is 'only Vaulting ambition' (ll.26–27).

4.2

a) 'It' is the assassination.

b) If the whole thing could be considered to be over and done with as soon as the deed was done, it would be better to do it quickly: that is, if the killing led to no difficult consequences but, with his death, only to success; if it were a self-contained action – in that case we could avoid all future problems.

c) The grammar of these first seven lines *is* confused, hesitant, then galloping – probably reflecting Macbeth's agitation and wishful thinking.

d) That those who live by the sword shall die by the sword – that, as Hamlet puts it, he might be 'hoist with his own petard' (Shakespeare, *Hamlet*, III, iv, 206), and have his evil plot rebound on him.

e) He is a good, virtuous, righteous king. The angels emphasise Duncan's goodness, in complete contrast to Macbeth's evil in killing him, which is 'The deep damnation of his taking-off' (l.20). It is a simple conflict between good and evil, which, reduced to its simplest terms, *Paradise Lost* is too.

f) 'Striding' (l.22), 'horsed' (l.22), 'couriers' (l.23), 'spur' (l.25), and perhaps 'o'erleaps ... And falls' (ll.27–28) if they are read as meaning one who mounts a horse too fast and falls on the other side. The impression is one of power, speed, authority, danger through recklessness.

g) It could be 'side', as in (f) above, echoing Macbeth's fear of a fall.

h) He is not yet ready and, in fact, does not do the deed until the next scene, after another soliloquy. After this present soliloquy, he suggests to Lady Macbeth that they should abandon the murder plot, but she convinces him that it must go ahead.

5.1 Text D Iris Murdoch, *The Sacred and Profane Love Machine*

(Luca is Harriet's young son.)

a) No reason is given. There is no evidence that anyone in the airport lounge has been deliberately chosen as a victim. The killing was therefore gratuitous. (It has no direct connection with anything else in the novel, either.)

b) 'A long glittering tube' (ll.13–14) and the 'crackling of deafening sound' (ll.17–18) suggest machine guns.

c) Open response. Newspaper reports could be used as contrast to or for comparison with Murdoch's narration. How effective is her style in making the scene real?

d) Open response.

5.2 a) and b) Students discuss their perceptions of the different styles of the passages. Asking them to choose sentences is simply a way of enabling them to focus on the task.

6 Simulation

Recommended duration: (a) 15 minutes
                (b) 30 minutes
                (c) 15 minutes
        Total 1 hour

Many students get very heated about this topic; the writing of notes on one's own opinions is a way of ensuring some order in the discussion. Some students might wish to opt out; they can make notes on what the others say in preparation for (c).

7 Violent language

a) Notice that 'blood' is not mentioned in these texts, until the very last words of the Murdoch text, when it comes as quite a shock. Rather the violence is described in a distanced way. It is this objectivity of description that is at the heart of the question. In sensational literature and journalism there is a kind of participation in the violence which borders on vicarious enjoyment of it. The following passage, taken from a popular daily newspaper, is useful in showing direct involvement in a violent scene.

> A war veteran with 10 medals was viciously scarred for life by two young thugs – for just £4. J.C., 60, was left unconscious and bleeding at a bus stop after the two-minute attack. His face was brutally slashed and the wounds needed 27 stitches. Last night at his home J.C. told of his nightmare after leaving a social club.
> "I was approached by a young man who asked me for the time. As soon as I looked at my watch another youth came from behind screaming 'We want your money.' I managed to punch one of them, but a knife was pulled out and blood seemed everywhere. Then I blacked out."

Contrast this with the anonymous, unsensational news item with the simple headline 'Rail death'.

> A middle-aged man was killed yesterday when he stepped into the path of the 10.36 Bognor Regis to Victoria train at West Green, West Sussex.

The first passage is, in a way, less shocking. The adverbs ('viciously', 'brutally') and heightened language ('scarred for life', 'nightmare') emphasise what is already a nasty story, but the second passage is somehow more effective in its understatement of the facts and its odd detailing of place names. Have students rewrite the second passage in the style of the first, and vice versa.

b) Use a story from local news which might be reported in a newspaper. On the basis of (a), students might be able to invent a story. The recounting of personal experience will have a different kind of subjectivity. Does the story seem less effective if narrated in the third person?

POSTSCRIPT

Man was born free, and everywhere he is in chains.

Jean-Jacques Rousseau, *The Social Contract*

8 Ideals

'Tis not too late to seek a newer world.

This unit is closely linked with Ambitions (Unit 9). Pre-presentation might be to examine the difference detween ideals and ambitions. The passages all deal with abstracts, intangibles, so it is necessary to keep close to the texts to avoid any danger of the discussions becoming too vague.

1.1 Theme

a) and b) Open response.

1.2 a) and b) Russell can certainly be called an idealist; his passage can almost be considered a definition of idealism. The 'upward' ideal relates to the positive side of human life – love and knowledge. It contrasts with pity for human suffering. Both sides of the coin are presented in the passages in this unit.

Try to end the discussion of the Russell passage on a positive note, to lead on to the texts.

2.1 Text A Rupert Brooke, *Heaven*

The tone of the poem (mock-seriousness) contrasts with that of the Russell passage and is brought out in the recording.

a) Yes. Lines 6 to 14 reflect human concerns about the hereafter and 'Mud unto mud' (l.15) echoes 'earth to earth, ashes to ashes, dust to dust' of the human committal service (from *The Book of Common Prayer*). Line 19 reflects eternal hopes for something better, and line 24 the benevolence of God, seen in fishy terms, but with words which echo the Biblical expression of human wishes.

b) The fish have just eaten, they are 'replete' (l.1) with flies and are relaxing at midday ('noon' l.2). The words indicate satiety and relaxation, so we can imagine that the fish are basically happy.

Ideals

c) Yes. See lines 9 (particularly) to 14.
d) He is eternal (l.20), very large, thinks like normal humble fish, and is physically like them with scales ('Squamous' (l.22)), and with the good qualities of the God of men. Religious echoes can be found in line 6 ('Beyond'), and the use of capital letters for words such as 'All' (l.7), 'Good' (l.9), and so on. Lines 11 to 13 are overtly religious. But then, 'To be at all is to be religious more or less', as Samuel Butler (1835–1902) said (*Notebooks*, 'Reconciliation: Religion'). This quotation might be used, now or later, as a stimulus for discussion.
e) More: water, mud, both of better quality (see l.18), a different kind of vegetation (l.27) (echoing the human idea that 'the other man's grass is always greener'), better food more easily found (ll.29–32). Above all less, indeed no, land, no threat contained in the attraction of insects, and no threat of dryness.

2.2 An exercise in Utopia-making. Short preliminary discussion before going into groups is useful. What would students do away with (how they would do away with them does not matter), what would they develop? Are the changes concerned almost exclusively with environment, or would human nature have to change too?

3.1 Text B Samuel Taylor Coleridge, *Kubla Khan* 📼

'Caverns measureless to man' (ll.4,27), 'a sunless sea' (l.5), 'that deep romantic chasm' (l.13), 'a waning moon' (l.15), 'a lifeless ocean' (l.28), 'war' (l.30), and 'ice' (ll.36,47) can all be interpreted as indicating something negative surrounding the positive, magical picture of the 'pleasure-dome'.

In the second part, 'once I saw' (l.38) and the continued idea of 'revive' (l.42) stress loss again. The poem is a delicate balance between the magic nature of the vision and the necessary loss of any such 'miracle of rare device' (l.35).

a) i) The area of Xanadu where the pleasure-dome was decreed.

ii) A circle five miles from side to side (both north to south and east to west).

iii) 'Incense-bearing' trees (l.9), 'forests' (l.10), and vegetation.

iv) 'Huge fragments' (l.21) and 'the sacred river' (l.24).

v) Lines 26 and 27.

vi) The distant sound of 'Ancestral voices prophesying war' (l.30).

vii) An emperor. He might be considered mythical by some students.

viii) 'Decree' shows Kubla Khan's power. 'So' (l.6) seems to imply that the decree was obeyed; what follows is the description of the 'stately pleasure-dome' (l.2) which resulted.

b) i) The poet.

ii) A vision of 'an Abyssinian maid' (l.39).

iii) To recall the *sound* of that vision. Because he would then, in 'deep delight' (l.44), be able to recreate the pleasure-dome.

iv) The result would be that everyone could see 'That sunny dome! those caves of ice!' (l.47) and would consider the poet a man enchanted, a man who had seen a vision of heaven and brought it back to earth.

v) He would have great power – if he were able to create such a dome.

vi) Because the poet would then be different from all the rest of mankind, to be held in 'holy dread' (l.52) and reverence.

vii) Some kind of perfect harmony of sight and sound.

3.2 a) and b) Coleridge's poetry is full of visual symbols. Here the ideas of perfection and symmetry are important; the map shows this. The map also brings out some of the opposites, or *polarities*, in the poem, together with the related idea of *completeness*: 'fountain' (l.19) / 'sunless sea' (l.5); 'caverns' (ll.4,27) / artificial 'caves' (ll.36,47); 'sunny spots of greenery' (l.11) / 'savage place' (l.14). The pleasure-dome, Kubla's work of art, contains all of these polarities – 'the mingled measure From the fountain and the caves' (ll.33–34).

The completed map will look something like this. Some students might prefer to see the whole thing as the pleasure-dome.

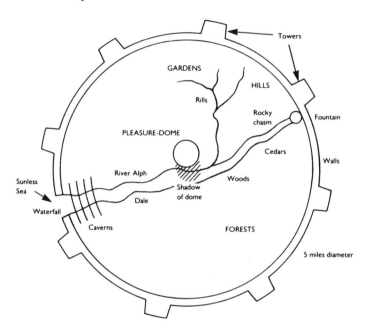

3.3 a) The 'pleasure-dome' (l.2) is a kind of perfection, both 'holy and enchanted' (l.14) (these adjectives qualify the 'savage place' (l.14) and the 'deep romantic chasm' of line 12, but by inference can be applied equally to the pleasure-dome), as is the vision of the 'damsel with a dulcimer' (l.37). The poet too would become 'holy and enchanted' if he could 'revive within' himself (l.42) the 'symphony and song' (l.43) of the vision.

b) Lines 42 to 49 are conditional – based on the hypothetical revival of the 'symphony and song' (l.43). The 'cry' (l.49) is in the present tense because the poet who had had such a vision would *now* be worthy of such reverence because of the fact of having fed 'on honey-dew' (l.53) 'And drunk the milk of Paradise' (l.54). If the poet had built 'that dome in air' (l.46) it could only have been through heavenly visions.

c) Many students will want to ignore the negative words in the poem. But they stress the limitations of the vision, the fact that it is a self-contained area (see 3.2). The vision of the 'damsel' too is circumscribed by its transitoriness, as the 'pleasure-dome' was by its topography. Both are as idealised as Brooke's fishy heaven.

4.1 **Text C** Charles Dickens, *Bleak House* 📼

'Telescopic Philanthropy' is apposite because of the distance involved, and also because the telescope seems to be the wrong way round – home has diminished to insignificance, while far-off Borrioboola-Gha looms very large, indeed exaggeratedly so. There are many examples of Mrs Jellyby's neglect , which will be enumerated in answer (e).

'Pattens' (ll.2,5) are overshoes, with thick soles, for housework or for walking in muddy streets.

a) The narrator is Miss (Esther) Summerson. She is not named until line 63. In line 7 we hear her described as one of 'two young ladies', the other of whom is named 'Ada' (l.6).

b) Caddy, the 'amanuensis' (l.79), and Peepy, who fell downstairs, are the only two of the 'several more' (l.8) actually named in the passage.

c) His counting of the bumps of Peepy's head on the stairs and landing (ll.13–15) and his quoted words in lines 18 and 19, 'As if ... they (Mrs Jellyby's eyes) could see nothing nearer than Africa'.

d) Among the possible descriptions are 'a lame invalid of a sofa' (l.25), 'her dress ... like a summer-house' (ll.29–31), all of the fifth paragraph (ll.32–37), 'such a state of ink' (l.41), the room's 'taste ... of hot tallow' (ll.47–48), the conversation about 'the climate' and 'Holborn' (ll.67–74), 'putting a number of papers towards us'(ll.75–76), 'to exhibit his wounded knees' (ll.92–93), and 'the bruises or the dirt' (l.94). Note Dickens's use of alliteration, as in lines 4–5. Students might find many more such examples, Dickens's humour being omnipresent.

e) The behaviour of the 'person in pattens' (ll.1–2), the 'several more children' (l.8), 'the dark' (l.9), Peepy's fall, the 'sofa' (l.25), Mrs Jellyby's hair (ll.25–27), her dress (ll.29–31), the 'room, which was strewn with papers' (l.32), 'similar litter' (l.33), the 'jaded and unhealthy' (l.38) look of Caddy and her 'state of ink' (l.41), in fact her whole description (ll.38–45, the 'taste ... of hot tallow' (ll.47–48), 'the fire' (l.48) and the 'ashes' (l.49), and the dismissal of Peepy (ll.95–96).

f) She is at first 'surprised' (l.4), then uneasy (ll.12–13), and then more and more 'struck' (l.38) by the curious and neglected state of things. She is then 'at a loss' (l.66) what to say to Mrs Jellyby and, in all, uncertain how to react.

g) The mentality which neglects home concerns, while claiming credit for useful work done abroad – self-absorption leading to neglect.

h) See introductory note on this passage.

4.2 Open response.

5.1 Text D Alfred, Lord Tennyson, *Ulysses*

Phrases which might be noted include lines 6, 22, 24–25, 26–28, 30–32, 52, 69–70. To 'drink life to the lees' means to enjoy life to the full until the last possible moment.

a) There is nothing to be gained in his present life, with an old wife, ruling people who do not know him (he was absent at Troy for a great many years).

b) Between great suffering and great joy, between solitude and loving company, between stormy sea and dry land.

c) 'I am become a name' (l.11), 'honour'd of them all' (l.15). Elicit whether students feel the use of 'am' in line 11 is more effective than the more usual 'have' would be.

d) Areas he himself has not visited but which call him onwards, and always will do so.

e) Not at all – he means that life is very much more than only to breathe.

f) Ulysses's life (one of the 'Life piled on life' (l.24)).

g) 'Every hour' (l.26). It is 'saved From that eternal silence' (ll.26–27) which death would bring, therefore it is exactly the opposite of death.

h) Lines 33 to 43 describe Telemachus as having qualities exactly the opposite of Ulysses – 'slow prudence' (l.36), 'soft degrees' (l.37), 'blameless' (l.39), 'decent' (l.40), tender and dutiful (ll.41–42). He is in no way negatively presented, but is perhaps the perfect Victorian governor, whereas Ulysses reflects the old Romantic of 'a frolic welcome' (l.47), a man 'that strove with Gods' (l.53).

i) Ulysses's 'mariners' (l.45). 'Opposed' (l.48) means they faced 'The thunder and the sunshine' (l.48) with their 'Free hearts, free foreheads'.

j) 'Work' (l.52).

k) To the 'friends' (l.56), his 'mariners' (l.45). He means launch the boat from the land, then row in their old order. 'Smite The sounding furrows' (ll.58–59) means use the oars upon the waves.

l) No. Their destination is indefinite in place and time.

m) Because their adventurous spirits, and their loyalty to Ulysses drive them on – there might always be 'a newer world' (l.57).

n) 'The long day' may indicate the evening on which they set sail, but it also contains the idea of Ulysses's long life nearing its end, yet still with the light of 'the slow moon' giving hope as it 'climbs', as he too can 'climb', 'strong in will' (l.69), though, as line 66 suggests, without the strength of earlier heroic days.

o) Open response. Do students hope they will still have questing spirits in old age – or would they prefer tranquillity and a settled life?

5.2 Ulysses and Russell share passions and have been blown hither and thither across the world. Their motivations were different, but their commitment very similar.

Students may wish to relate:

– Ulysses's wish to explore unknown lands to Coleridge's predilection for imaginary worlds;
– Ulysses's wish to 'escape' from the present world to Mrs Jellyby's neglect of domestic matters;
– Russell's strong passion to Coleridge's;
– Russell's constant awareness of suffering in the world, and his conviction that he cannot 'alleviate the evil', with Mrs Jellyby's efforts to do good while remaining unaware of suffering at home.

6 Simulation

This builds on the exercise in Utopia-building in 2.2 (c), taking the final choice of ideal world (the best one to live in rather than the easiest to believe in) as its basis.

Recommended duration:	(a)–(b)	Individual	15 minutes
	(c)	Pair work	10 minutes
	(d)	Individual	5 minutes
	(e)	Class	30 minutes? (duration depends on class size)
	(f)	Individual (homework?)	30 minutes
		Total	1 hour 30 minutes

7 The language of ideals

The list will be long. For single words, get students to find less extreme synonyms. How would their contexts differ? 'Seek' is more abstract than the more mundane 'look for'.

POSTSCRIPT

After all has been said that can be said about the widening influence of ideas, it remains true that they would hardly be such strong agents unless they were taken in a solvent of feeling. The great world-struggle of developing thought is continually foreshadowed in the struggle of the affections, seeking a justification for love and hope.

George Eliot, *Romola*

9 Ambitions

What's a heaven for?

Thematically this is one of the simpler units, but one which calls for considerable investment of personal views, feelings, and desires by students. It ties in closely with Unit 8, Ideals; Unit 6 on Indifference will be a useful counterpoint. The texts show the range of ambitions from the simple and mundane, to the universal.

1.1 Theme

The two quotations show the range.

Peter Tinniswood, *I Didn't Know You Cared*
'Rabbiting away like buggery' is a Northern English turn of phrase which will probably not be found in any dictionary. It means simply (but graphically) 'chattering incessantly'. 'Me' and 'nowt' are dialect forms for 'my' and 'nothing'. This is a kind of 'power' ambition. Elicit what kind of 'magic power' students would like to have, if they could. Discuss the need for this kind of 'escape-valve' fantasy, especially in crowded places (trains, buses, traffic, queues, etc.).

Christopher Marlowe, *Tamburlaine*
Marlowe describes the four elements (air, earth, water, fire) within the human soul. He echoes Doctor Faustus's quest for 'knowledge infinite' and suggests we should 'wear ourselves, and never rest' (l.9) until we reach the summit of our ambitions, 'an earthly crown' (l.12), mastery or complete fulfilment in success on earth. Students' conception of ambition will be more limited, possibly more mundane – but elicit whether their wildest dreams of fame, wealth, success, do not resemble Marlowe's description a little.

1.2 Open response

1.3 Apart from providing and eliciting useful vocabulary, this activity enlarges ideas on the topic; it is especially useful following the discussion of personal experiences of ambitions.

2.1 **Text A** Robert Browning, *Andrea del Sarto* 📼

The poem is sub-titled *(Called 'The Faultless Painter')*. It is a dramatic monologue, addressed to the 'Lucrezia' mentioned in line 11. So the speaker's profession is painter. Andrea del Sarto was in fact a Florentine painter, whose real name was Andrea Vannucchi and who lived from 1486 to 1531. Vasari was among his pupils.

The contrast within the poem is between craftsmanship, flawless perfection without inspiration, and inspiration which creates works less technically perfect but more lasting, more attractive. 'Morello' (l.26) is a reference to the horse of Lorenzo the Magnificent (1449–1492), the last great Medici ruler of Florence in the fifteenth century.

a) Being an accomplished painter (see line 7, 'To paint a little thing like that').

b) The 'twenty such' (l.4) 'Who strive' (l.6) 'To paint a little thing' (l.7). They 'do much less, so much less ... so much less!' (ll.9–10) than Andrea del Sarto, but he feels 'judged' (l.11) and their 'less is more' (l.11).

c) Craftsmanship is 'less' (ll.9,10) than 'a truer light of God' (l.12) which burns in the others 'Who strive' (l.6) – this is the contrast between technique (Andrea) and inspiration (the others).

d) That he is uninspired while his works *seem* inspired. He knows they are not greatly inspired because he paints 'from myself and to myself' (l.23), but the resultant works, with great craftsmanship and technique can seem 'nearer heaven' (l.20) than they, or he, are.

e) 'The mountain' is an object, huge on the landscape, which cannot be ignored but, being inanimate, cannot be moved emotionally or touched by worldly things. Andrea himself is the mountain for this moment.

f) No. He works precisely within 'his grasp', not aiming beyond his limitations, remaining 'Placid' (l.32) like his work.

g) Because, in some ways, it would be better to overreach himself, to run risks, try the unknown, instead of remaining predictable and perfect.

h) He is resigned but still feels 'the worse' (l.32) for his lack of inspiration.

2.2 Open response. Most people do not try to overcome their limitations to any notable degree, preferring the safety of the known to the risks of the unknown. Why should it be different for an artist?

When we are young we often have 'vaulting ambition', as Macbeth describes it. With maturity this lessens, and our ambitions assume a more reasonable tone. Will limitations restrict the achievement of the wildest dreams mentioned earlier?

Do students react to criticism by wanting to give up, or by trying to do better? Is this outside influence a good or bad thing? Ambitious people are often selfish, arrogant, over-assertive, pushy. Is this a necessary part of the ability to be successful?

2.3 Elicit any experience of 'perfect' works of art and compare/contrast them with less perfect but more inspired works. Have students found any examples of perfection or inspiration in this book?

The Ruskin quote confirms Browning's last two lines, implying that the artist must always be more than just a craftsman. Do students share this feeling? Is Oscar Wilde's statement (in the Preface to *The Picture of Dorian Gray*) that 'All art is quite useless' true? Or is it countered by Keats's 'A thing of beauty is a joy forever' (*Endymion*) and 'Beauty is truth, truth beauty' (*Ode on a Grecian Urn*)? Perhaps it is also worth recalling here Samuel Butler's words in *Erewhon*: 'An art can only be learned in the workshop of those who are winning their bread by it'.

3.1 Text B Oscar Wilde, *The Picture of Dorian Gray*

a) Sybil Vane's vision of Jim in Australia is obviously fantastical and impossible. It contains a number of romantic adjectives which show this exaggeration: 'the *wonderful* heiress' (ll.5–6), 'the *wicked* ... bushrangers' (ll.6–7), '*immense* slaughter' (l.21), etc. The fantasy is almost traditional – the hero overcomes all manner of monsters and vicissitudes, to end up 'rich', 'happy', and to get the girl at the end of it all. Realistic touches only add to the fantasy, rather than reduce its marvellousness.

b) Open response. The fantasy has its attractive points, but like all such 'castles in the air' it brings you 'down with a bump' when you return to reality.

c) The 'bushrangers' (ll.7,19), shipboard life etc., and 'the gold-fields' (ll.15,22), described as 'horrid places' (l.22), are all negative fantasies which confirm Sybil's complete ignorance of reality. What the positive and negative fantasies have in common is that she imagines everything as if it were a story-book romance where good and bad are clearly defined and all comes out well at the end.

d) She cares about Jim, but knows very little about him (or she would not be fantasising a life for him) or about Australia, or about human nature, or about life. Her faith in God ('God was very good, and would watch over him', ll.36–37) is rather childish – that perhaps sums her up. 'She knew so much more of life' (33–34) is patently false.

3.2 Fantasies often equate wealth with happiness. We do not all, like Shylock, 'dream of money-bags' (*The Merchant of Venice*, II v 17), but probably few of us would refuse to be comfortably off. The Beatles' song (Money) 'Can't Buy Me Love' is relevant here too. How much (money, or anything else) would students really want? Recall another line from *The Merchant of Venice*: 'They are as sick that surfeit with too much, As they that starve with nothing' (I ii 5–6).

4.1 Text C Thomas Gray, *Elegy Written in a Country Churchyard*

Throughout *Reading between the lines*, students have worked on extracts, with all the attendant problems, the main one being the danger of distortion and misinterpretation caused by the absence of the whole context. Here, the whole of Gray's poem is given, but broken up into seven more readily assimilable sections. Students read silently, in groups or individually, and attempt to answer the questions that follow their section. The 'jigsaw' is then put together as a kind of discovery of how each part, in sequence, fits to make the whole poem. Students will listen to the whole poem at 4.3, after the groups have reported on their sections.

Group 1
a) The poet is speaking in a churchyard, near the church 'tow'r' (l.9), under the trees (l.13). It is sunset.
b) The sounds of an insect (l.7) and of sheep-bells (l.8), and the ·sound of an owl (l.10) who is herself disturbed by 'such, as

(are) wand'ring near her ... bow'r' (l.11): the poet for example.
c) 'Each' (l.15) of 'The rude Forefathers of the hamlet' (l.16).
d) 'The rude Forefathers of the hamlet' (l.16).

Group 2
Since their first verse says what will happen 'For them' (l.21) and the second verse tells what they did, it can be deduced that they are dead. Line 38 mentions 'their Tomb', and line 36 'the grave', so it is clear that the lives of the dead 'poor' (l.32) are the poet's concern. They were humble ('homely' (l.30)), hard-working. Lines 33 to 36 speak in general – everyone, great or humble, must die. Lines 39 and 40 imply both the church and the island of Great Britain (aisle/'isle' play on words).

Group 3
a) The impossibility of a return from the dead.
b) A churchyard, possibly in the country.
c) 'Some heart' (l.46) and 'Hands' (l.47).
d) The people in the graves are anonymous, their potential having remained undiscovered. The other verses show examples of possible ('pregnant' (l.46)) power (l.47) and poetic achievement (l.48) whilst also showing how these villagers' limitations were 'repress'd' (l.51) and they were thereby rendered anonymous.
e) All were great or famous men, in history or literature. (Their greatness is, in this context, more important than who they were or what they did, but students might want to find out more about them from reference books.) They are mentioned to contrast with the anonymity of the local dead, who might have shared these great men's potential.

Group 4
a) Line 65 – 'forbad'.
b) 'Forbad' (l.67).
c) 'These bones' (l.77) is the only reference this group can use.
d) The second 'Forbad' (l.67), introducing the evils that these people were excluded from, compensates for the great things (ll.61–64) denied to them.
e) 'Virtues' and 'crimes' (l.66) respectively (and together).
f) Limited, unambitious, rough.

Group 5
a) The 'bones' (l.77) and 'memorial' (l.78) possibly suggest that he is in a churchyard.

b) Simple inscriptions on tombstones.
c) 'Left' (l.87) and 'cast' (l.88). 'Who' (l.85) is the subject. 'Nor cast' (l.88) means 'without casting'.
d) Those who 'resigned' 'This pleasing anxious being' (l.86) – i.e. those who die. They look back at life, reluctant ('ling'ring') to leave it.
e) Yes. Someone left behind ('some fond breast' (l.89)) for the dying one's support and comfort and 'Some pious drops' (l.90), or tears, are described, in the choice of verbs 'relies' (l.89) and 'requires' (l.90), as necessary.

Group 6
a) The poet and the poem.
b) The poet.
c) Almost the traditional picture of a poet, distracted, strange, different, as if mad.
d) He describes him quite fondly but dispassionately, as a normal part of the landscape, nothing special, but 'miss'd' (l.109) when he was not there. There is a touch of respect in lines 115 and 116 for 'the lay'.
e) The Swain himself cannot read, but 'thou' (l.115) can. 'Thou' refers directly to 'Some kindred Spirit' (l.96) (and possibly, by analogy, to the poet and/or the reader).

Group 7
a) On a gravestone.
b) An unknown young man who lived a sad, lonely life.
c) No.
d) Goodness and sincerity.

4.2 Each group will take a few minutes (not too long) to work out its own answers. As reporting back goes on, there will be the temptation for later groups to adjust their answers. Insist on the original (uninfluenced) answers first, then adjustments if there are any. The poem will emerge as first local, then generalising while remaining local, always respectful, ending with the personal note of the poet's own epitaph. Attitudes to life and death are the basic subject matter of the poem – is ambition useless if 'The paths of glory lead but to the grave' (l.36)? Or is Marlowe's 'earthly crown' (see 1.1) worth working towards?

4.3 a) It is not happy as such, but few will find it very sad.

b) No.

c) He appears not to be.

5 Simulation

Recommended duration: (a) 10 minutes
(b) 10 minutes
(c) 15 minutes
(d) 20 minutes
Total 55 minutes

This does more than any other simulation in the book to relate personal attitudes to the unit topic, and to bring differences in attitudes to the surface. Previous work on the texts has already prepared students, as in other units, to be aware of their own views on the topic.

6 The language of determination

Help the class by asking direct questions such as:
'Can you remember a time when you had to be very *firm*? Describe the situation. What did you say? How did you say it?'
'Have you ever been *half-hearted* about anything? How did your speech show it?'
(cf. Unit 8, Ideals, p.80)

POSTSCRIPT

Ambition is the last refuge of the failure.

Oscar Wilde, *Phrases and Philosophies for the Use of the Young*

10 Meaning

What does it mean? he says – What's it meant to mean?

This unit is the last, and should be taught last, because student response to it will be richer after reading and discussing the other texts in the book – and also because it directs *conscious* attention to the concept of levels of meaning. It sets out to *question* meaning, to show ranges and possibilities of meaning together with ranges and possibilities of the *expression* of meaning – from Wilde's *The Importance of Being Earnest* to Edwin Morgan's *Message Clear*.

You may find it useful and interesting, before beginning the unit, to have students read and discuss what a number of writers have said on the subject of meaning:

Words are, of course, the most powerful drug used by mankind.

Rudyard Kipling (in a speech)

'Then you should say what you mean,' the March Hare went on. 'I do,' Alice hastily replied; 'at least – at least I mean what I say – that's the same thing, you know'

Lewis Carroll, *Alice in Wonderland*

I don't mean anything. Why should I?

D.H. Lawrence, *Women in Love*

Be sure that you go to the author to get at *his* meaning, not to find yours.

John Ruskin, *Sesame and Lilies*

All meanings, we know, depend on the key of interpretation.

George Eliot, *Daniel Deronda*

1.1 Theme

The illustrations show that one way of looking at meaning is as a function of the relationship between text and reader/listener.

74

See the quotation from *Daniel Deronda* above. The references to activities in *Reading between the lines* show that there are infinite ways of 'getting at' meaning, and that students have used many of them in working through this book.

1.2 You might wish to introduce the idea of 'underlying discourse'. The underlying discourse of most advertisements is 'Buy this'; of most politicians 'Vote for me' or 'My opponent is wrong'. In personal terms, 'I'm sorry' may or may not mean what it says, depending on a range of variables (who says it, to whom, when, why, etc.). H.G. Widdowson's example 'The door is open' can be used as a further example. It may mean 'Close it', 'Go away', 'Come in', 'People outside can overhear us', 'Why is it open?', 'I told you to close it', and so on.

We do not always say what we mean for many reasons. Sometimes we do not think it necessary, as in the Widdowson example, because the context makes it clear (and sometimes we are wrong to think so!); politeness or embarrassment may limit us, uncertainty or inadequacy may inhibit us, we may not find the right words, etc., etc. There are endless reasons – it makes us wonder if we ever succeed in saying exactly what we mean! Anyway, is it clear that we *know* what we mean when we speak?

2.1 Text A   Oscar Wilde, *The Importance of Being Earnest*

The term 'underlying discourse' might be introduced here if it hasn't already been mentioned. Gwendolen's first speech and Cecily's second actually mean 'You are quite wrong', and this meaning continues to underlie their speeches until they speak to themselves (ll.26–34). The first exchange casts aspersions on each girl's social status and experience. Only the aside 'Detestable girl' really reveals Gwendolen's feelings. Cecily's outburst in her second-last speech is amply covered by her final very polite-seeming, but definitive lines.

a) 'Miss' lends a more formal distance to the conversation at moments when Cecily and Gwendolen are at odds with one another.

b) The diaries provide written confirmation of the 'engagements', and also reveal the girls' habit of writing down the events of their lives every day. Gwendolen's line is one of Wilde's most famous witticisms, echoing the Victorian fashion for reading detective stories and the like while travelling by train. It is most unlikely that Gwendolen's

diary will actually contain anything that could truly be
described as 'sensational'.

c) Cecily's wish to confide the news of her engagement and
Gwendolen's polite reaction; Gwendolen's reaction to the
mention of a spade, and her questions about walks and
flowers, as well as her criticism of country life underline her
town-bred superiority and point up the basic conflict
between the two characters.

d) 'Manners' are maintained with a veneer of politeness but, by
the end of the scene, it is clear that venom vanquishes
veneer, and the mask is seen to have been shallow indeed.

e) '... widely different' (l.46), 'I hate crowds' (l.63), 'Oh,
flowers are as common ...' (ll.75–76), 'agricultural de-
pression' (l.82), and many more. Students might enjoy
re-hearing and discussing intonation patterns and the
emphases given to such words.

f) They underline the falsity of the characters' politeness to
each other, and then reinforce the point-scoring element in
the ensuing battle of wits and words.

2.2 Open response.

3.1 **Text B** Jane Austen, *Emma* 🔊

'Courtship' comes from the first two lines of the 'Charade'
describing 'My first' – court; 'my second' is 'the monarch of the
seas' – a ship. 'Courtship' ('united') brings man to his knees in
the service of women. The last two lines show that the riddle
itself seeks 'approval' for just such a union in courtship.

a) Students can attempt to work out the relationship. Answering (b) – (d) will gradually clarify it.

b) Three: Mr Elton, Miss Woodhouse (Emma), and Miss Smith
(Harriet). 'A friend' is a fabrication.

c) He is in love with Emma. Emma wants to bring him and
Harriet together, so she (Emma) does not see the true object
of the 'Charade'; Harriet is meanwhile 'in a tremor' because
she believes Emma's idea that Mr Elton really loves her.

d) Emma has no idea that Mr Elton loves her. Jane Austen
gives us the hint at 'he stopped a moment' (l.21) when Mr
Elton names Miss Woodhouse, and later in his seemingly
innocuous words 'I do not offer it for Miss Smith's collection' (l.29) and 'The speech was more to Emma than to

Harriet' (l.32). The irony is that Emma should read first a 'Charade' intended for herself, believing it to be for Harriet.

3.2 Open response.

4.1 Text C Samuel Beckett, *Happy Days*

Students will of course have their own ideas, but the pre-question is a 'catch' question: Winnie is not really talking to anyone, not even Willie. She is chattering to herself and is 'Thankful' (l.28) for anything she can find or remember ('The old style', l.2) that she can chatter about. The audience is eavesdropping.

a) They are negative words, implying that Winnie thought Mr Shower or Cooker was talking rubbish. (The qualification 'usual' (l.12) implies that everyone who sees Winnie – the audience in the theatre too, perhaps? – says something similar about her and her strange situation.)

b) Having filed the nails of her left hand she looks better, looks 'a bit more human'.

c) *grips* cases (they are soft-sided travelling bags rather than suitcases)

   gaping staring, open-mouthed

   stake bet

   diddies breasts, bosom

   ditty bag (originally a fisherman's or sailor's bag; nothing to do with ditty = song)

   muck dirt (here it is probably food; Beckett's characters often have a penchant for tinned food, cf. *Theatre One*)

   fornicating fucking (as expletive; fornicating is usually used as a synonym for copulating)

d) Because the woman's use of bad language makes Winnie judge her a 'coarse creature' (l.17) and therefore a suitable partner for the man described as 'coarse fellow' (ll.10–11).

e) Willie. Referred to as 'he' by Mr Shower or Cooker.

f) 'No, done him'. No, I've already filed that nail. Almost all Winnie's phrases can be filled out in this way – usually the subject is missing, or the connectors, so that it might seem difficult to follow Winnie's thoughts.

g) 'It' is the memory of the visit of the Showers or Cookers who were the last people she saw. (The cohesive reference is to 'thing' in line 27). Because it gives her something to talk about.

Meaning

4.2   Students will have their own ideas, and there might be many. Point out that some people will never be content to leave an image as it stands, and enjoy it, reflect on it, without being tempted to attribute 'meaning' to it. It *could* represent Winnie's atrophy, the stagnancy of life in middle-age (Winnie is about fifty), lack of communication, or sex, in her marriage, the repetitiveness and static nature of most lives, and so on. The image will evoke impressions in an audience's mind which are very similar to the connotations that words may evoke, only on a deeper and more wide-ranging scale.

It is important to distinguish between the image and the connotations or implications of the image. The word 'symbol' should be avoided unless with reference to the specific use of an object or reference to stand in an emblematic way for something greater.

5 Text D   Edwin Morgan, *Message Clear*

For obvious reasons, this text is not recorded on the cassette. The poem is not as difficult as it looks and is, in fact, quite entertaining to work through letter by letter. It will confirm the range of variations on how meaning is achieved, hidden, exploited, clouded, doubled, and generally played with by writers. The full text, rendered in words but with no punctuation, is:

Am I if I am he hero hurt there and here and here and there I am rife in Sion and I die a mere sect a mere section of the life of men sure the die is set and I am the surd at rest O life I am here I act I run I meet I tie I stand I am Thoth I am Ra I am the sun I am the son I am the erect one if I am rent I am safe I am sent I heed I test I read a thread a stone a tread a throne I resurrect a life I am in life I am resurrection I am the resurrection and I am I am the resurrection and the life

Students might enjoy putting in some punctuation, and seeing how it affects meaning.

a) Religious references, and the continued use of 'I', make it possible to interpret the speaker throughout as Christ. In this case, the early lines are about the Crucifixion. 'The die is set' (ll.22–24) means that he has taken an incontrovertible step. 'A thread' (l.45) to 'a throne' (l.48) gives the only very obvious rhyme in the poem, effective in its absence of 'I' just before the final clear message.

b) The words as written out baldly are unsatisfying. The working-out of what the poem is about is like the speaker's struggling through all kinds of difficulties to his final realisation.

Message Clear

Lines
1–4	Am I, if I am he, hero?
5–10	Hurt there and here and here and there
11–14	I am rife in Sion and I die
15–20	A mere sect, a mere section of the life of men
21–24	Sure, the die is set and
25–26	I am the surd at rest
27–28	O life, I am here
29–33	I act, I run, I meet, I tie, I stand
34–35	I am Thoth, I am Ra
36–37	I am the sun, I am the son
38–39	I am the erect one, if I am rent
40–41	I am safe, I am sent
42–44	I heed, I test, I read
45–46	A thread, a stone
47–48	A tread, a throne
49–50	I resurrect a life
51	I am in life
52	I am resurrection
53–54	I am the resurrection and I am
55	I am the resurrection and the life

c) Open response. Edwin Morgan called it a poem. What else could it be called? This should make students reflect on the forms of poetry – as rigid as the sonnet, as experimental as *Message Clear*. (Morgan's work is usually described as 'concrete poetry', but the term is now rather out of favour.)
d) Perhaps because the message is finally clear (in the last line), although, like a railway station announcement board, or a telescreen word processor, or a telex printout (which it resembles in part), the message has at first seemed unclear.
e) It should be different, clearer, and probably more meaningful on re-reading.
f) By now it is not for us, or the teacher, to say! You could refer to the unit's postscript at this point.

6 Simulation

Recommended duration: 1 hour 30 minutes

Students are now required to read, as readers of literature, for pleasure and a well-defined purpose. You will find that they spend most of the allotted time discussing ways in which the poems convey their meanings, and which does it most effectively. Note that the uniting theme of the five poems is 'expressing meanings in words'.

It is important that students get to the point of announcing and comparing their results; the group work should come to an end after an hour or one hour 15 minutes at the most. Do not reveal the names of the authors, though you might wish to do so on completion of the activity.

When we were young	Arthur Harvey
Opening the cage	Edwin Morgan
Contact	Roy Boardman
On no work of words	Dylan Thomas
Arrival	John McRae

POSTSCRIPT

Even when poetry has a meaning, as it usually has, it may be inadvisable to draw it out ... Perfect understanding will sometimes almost extinguish pleasure.

A.E. Housman, *The Name and Nature of Poetry*

Appendix: The authors

W.H. (Wystan Hugh) AUDEN (1907–1973). Born in England, he took American citizenship in middle life. Famous for his left-wing poetry in the 1930s he also wrote plays with Christopher Isherwood. He developed into one of the greatest poets and critics of the century. *Musée des Beaux Arts* belongs to the mid-1930s.

Jane AUSTEN (1775–1817) was the greatest writer on English society and manners at the end of the eighteenth century. Observing her limited sphere with supreme wit and elegance of style, she has left us a complete picture of a world and a fascinating range of characters. *Emma* (1816) was one of only six novels she wrote, *Northanger Abbey, Sense and Sensibility, Pride and Prejudice, Mansfield Park,* and *Persuasion* being the others.

Samuel BECKETT (born 1906), like his mentor and friend James Joyce, left his native Ireland to write, and since the early 1930s has lived in France. One of the most important novelists and playwrights of the century, he was awarded the Nobel Prize for Literature in 1969. *Happy Days* dates from 1961.

Roy BOARDMAN (born 1937) studied at the universities of London and Essex, then taught English and Drama at secondary schools. Since 1965 he has taught at schools and universities in Italy, and is at present Director of the British Council in Naples. Apart from various textbooks and articles on language and literature teaching, he has published stories and poems.

BOSTON WOMEN'S COLLECTIVE was a group of feminists whose consciousness-raising work resulted in the publication of the massive volume *Our Bodies Ourselves* (1971) which had worldwide success and influenced a whole generation of women.

Rupert BROOKE (1887–1915) became famous, especially after his death, as one of the golden generation killed in the First World War. His poetry was of various kinds, from the experimentally realistic to the nostalgic, sentimental, and patriotic. *Heaven* is unusually ironic. He is much more a 'modern' than a 'Georgian' poet, despite the critical categorisation of him as such.

Appendix: The authors

Robert BROWNING (1812–1889). A great and original poet, whose work has always been controversial, Browning never achieved the success of his contemporary Tennyson, although his *Men and Women* (1855) and *Dramatis Personae* (1864) established him as the absolute master of the dramatic monologue form, in which characters (Andrea del Sarto, for example), both real and imagined, reveal themselves in their own words. He was married to Elizabeth Barrett.

Lewis CARROLL (1832–1898) was the pen name of Charles Lutwidge Dodgson, a mathematician and man of religion best known for his fantasy novels which contain complex patterns of sense and nonsense befitting a man whose professional concerns in an age of doubt and uncertainty lay between logic and religion. He was a great inventor of words, an experimenter with sounds and associations. *Alice's Adventures in Wonderland* (1865) and *Through the Looking Glass* (1872) are perennial favourites.

Kate CHOPIN (1851–1904), better known as a short story writer, was the author of one major novel, *The Awakening* (1899), which reflects her psychological insight, especially into female characters, and her mastery of description of the New Orleans area where she spent most of her life.

Winston CHURCHILL (1874–1965), statesman and writer, Prime Minister of Great Britain 1940–1945 and 1951–1955.

John CLARE (1793–1864) is one of the great poets of the English countryside. Always very poor, he became celebrated in the 1820s as part of the fashion for country works. From 1837 he was kept in Northampton Lunatic Asylum suffering from delusions, and there he went on writing, much of his verse touching on his loneliness, and his deprivation of genius in a social system which exploited his natural talents.

Samuel Taylor COLERIDGE (1772–1834) was one of the most interesting poets of all time. He is best known for his collaboration with William Wordsworth on *Lyrical Ballads* (1798), which contained *The Rime of the Ancient Mariner*. *Kubla Khan* (1816) was allegedly written under the influence of opium – and was interrupted by the arrival of a 'person from Porlock' – but it can be seen to be complete as it stands. Coleridge was also a great critic and talker. *Biographia Letteraria* (1817) contains most of his philosophical theories on art and the artist. Considered a 'Romantic', he is difficult to contain in one definition.

William COWPER (1731–1800) is a strange figure in eighteenth century poetry. He would probably now be described as manic depressive, but despite this recurring illness he produced volumes of poems and hymns, his masterpiece being the blank-verse long poem *The Task* (1785) which was very successful in its rendering of his main preoccupation, the beauty of nature as an escape from corrupt reality – reflected also in *The Poplar Field*. His letters reveal him as a complex and fascinating character, of greater interest than his poems might indicate.

Charles DICKENS (1812–1870) is one of the greatest novelists in the English language. His distinctive humour, an immortal range of characters, and wide-ranging development of themes have led him to be called 'the Shakespeare of the novel'. *Bleak House* was first published in serial form in 1852–53 and *Hard Times* in 1854.

Emily DICKINSON (1830–1886) lived a quiet life in Amherst, Massachusetts, producing a remarkable quantity of verse (some 1775 poems) which was not published until after her death. Her style is idiosyncratic and intense, a reflection of her complex and reclusive personality, but her poems have a freshness, innovativeness, and humour which have given her a very high standing as an early modernist.

George ELIOT (1819–1880) was the pseudonym of Mary Ann (or Marian) Evans. She came to writing novels after a long period as a translator and reviewer. Her greatest work, *Middlemarch* (1871–72), remains one of the most significant novels in the English language, the fruit of a long period of painstaking research and refinement of technique which had produced such well-known works as *Adam Bede, Silas Marner,* and *Romola*.

Frederick FORSYTH (born 1938) was a well-known journalist who brought his documentary and investigative style to the genre of semi-factual adventure thrillers, such as *The Day of the Jackal* (1971), *The Odessa File* (1972), and *The Dogs of War* (1974).

Thomas GRAY (1716–1771) is best known for his *Elegy*, written between 1747 and 1750 and set in Stoke Poges, Buckinghamshire, where the famous graveyard can still be seen. Despite his small output, Gray was offered the poet laureateship in 1757, but refused it. His handling of the themes of history and death made him one of the most influential voices of the eighteenth century.

Appendix: The authors

Arthur (Edward) HARVEY (1904–1983) was an educationalist and
poet. Although he lived and worked in Paraguay, Paris, Italy,
Northern Ireland and Essex, he never left his native Cornwall in spirit,
and it was there that he wrote some of his best poems, which appeared
in many journals and in his Cornish collection, *The Land's End
Peninsula*.

Joseph HELLER (born 1923) has written several novels, but will be
remembered for *Catch-22* (1961), the most brilliant comic novel to
come out of the Second World War. The idea of the 'catch', which
represents the individual's constant difficulties in the face of bureau-
cratic authoritarian logic, has now become part of the English
language.

Christopher ISHERWOOD (born 1904) a very fine documentary
novelist and, at the same time, the best homosexual writer in
English. His fame came from his Berlin novels, *Mr Norris Changes
Trains* (1935) and *Goodbye to Berlin* (1939), which inspired the
musical and film 'Cabaret'. He has continued to write in his
well-known 'I am a camera' style, his more recent works including
Down There on a Visit (1962) and his masterpiece *A Single Man*
(1964).

Philip LARKIN (born 1922), one of the most highly regarded living
English poets, works as a librarian in Hull, and has a remarkably
small collection of slim volumes of verse to his credit. These,
however, have established him as a brilliant social observer and
commentator on ordinary life. His works include two novels – *Jill*
(1946) and *A Girl in Winter* (1947) – and verse – *The North Ship*
(1945), *The Less Deceived* (1955), *The Whitsun Weddings* (1964),
High Windows (1979) – and criticism – *Required Writing* (1983).

D.H. (David Herbert) LAWRENCE (1885–1930), the son of a Notting-
hamshire coal miner, was one of the first writers to express the
conflicts of the emergence of the artist from a working class
background. He wrote novels, short stories, poetry, plays, essays,
criticism, and letters, while constantly travelling the world over in
search of his ideal, his perfection of life. *Sons and Lovers*, his third
novel, was published in 1913.

Konrad LORENZ (born 1903) has become world famous for his work
on animal behaviour, principally at the Austrian Academy of
Sciences. His writings have brought his work to a wide audience –
King Solomon's Ring (1952), *Man Meets Dog* (1954), *Studies in
Animal and Human Behaviour* (1970), and *Civilized Man's Eight
Deadly Sins* (1974) are the best known. He won the Nobel Prize for
Physiology/Medicine in 1973.

Christopher MARLOWE (1564–1593). The greatest English play-
wright before Shakespeare, his works are the high point of a
rhetorical, classically influenced style. *Tamburlaine*, in two parts
(c.1587), was his first great success, to be followed by *Doctor
Faustus*, *The Jew of Malta*, and other plays, as well as a number of
very fine poems. He was murdered in a tavern brawl involving
government spies.

Ian McEWAN (born 1948) is one of the liveliest of the new generation
of writers. His works show a fascination for the corrupt and gory,
which some readers find distressing. *Dead As They Come* is from
his second collection of stories, *In Between the Sheets* (1978). His
other works include *First Love, Last Rites* (1975) and two novels,
The Cement Garden (1978) and *The Comfort of Strangers* (1981).

John McRAE (born 1949) studied at the Universities of Glasgow and
Nottingham, then worked for the British Council for five years. He
has taught in several southern Italian universities since 1975. Apart
from his work on the integration of language and literature studies,
he has published articles on Shakespeare, Dickens, George Eliot,
D.H. Lawrence, modern drama, cultural studies, and theatre
workshop techniques, as well as several textbooks.

John MILTON (1608–1674) was equally well known as a pamphleteer
and as a poet, commenting throughout his life on the social and
historical questions of a tumultuous period in British history.
Paradise Lost (1667) is his greatest work in verse.

Edwin MORGAN (born 1920), formerly Professor of English at the
University of Glasgow, became one of the foremost 'concrete' poets,
and has also translated many European poets into English. His
Collected Poems was published in 1982.

Iris MURDOCH (born 1919) is a prolific novelist in the Anglo-Irish
tradition, whose background as a university philosopher imbues her
novels with an intelligence and thematic complexity that sets her
above most modern writers. *The Sacred and Profane Love Machine*
was published in 1974.

Joe ORTON (1933–1967) was killed by his male lover at the height of
his fame, having written a handful of anarchic black farces which
place him high in the pantheon of English comic writers, among
such names as Congreve and Wilde. His attacks on authority and
institutions reflect the struggle of a social outcast to make sense of a
hypocritical society. *Loot* was first performed in 1966.

George ORWELL (1903–1950) was the pseudonym of Eric Blair, one
of England's most politically committed writers, although he was
never a member of any political party. His most famous works,

Animal Farm (1945) and *Nineteen Eighty-Four* (1949), display his ability to render in terms of fable his deep convictions against political indoctrination.

Wilfred OWEN (1893–1918) is now the best known of the World War One poets. He was encouraged to write by another poet, Siegfried Sassoon, who collected his poems for publication in 1920. His was a new voice, sharply realistic, technically assured, unromantic and unheroic, a voice which had a profound influence on the generations which followed him.

Coventry PATMORE (1823–1896) was very much a minor poet of the Victorian Age, but his four-volume *Angel in the House* (1854–62) is marvellously representative of the values of the time, being a straightforward celebration of conjugal love in simple language and verse forms. He worked for nearly twenty years in the Printed Book Department of the British Museum.

Harold PINTER (born 1930) has established his own particular style in modern theatre through such successes as *The Birthday Party, The Caretaker, Landscape* and *Silence,* and *Betrayal. A Night Out* was first produced on radio and television in 1960.

Isaac ROSENBERG (1890–1918) is considered by many to be an even greater poet than Wilfred Owen, his war poems being extraordinarily direct and honest. His poetry was collected by Gordon Bottomley in 1922, but it was not until recently that he came to be regarded as a major figure.

Bertrand RUSSELL (1872–1970). A philosopher and mathematician, he became Earl Russell in 1931. He won the Nobel Prize for Literature in 1950 for his voluminous writings on education, philosophy, ethics, and pacifism, to name but a few of the subjects which attracted his interests. His *Autobiography* appeared in three volumes between 1967 and 1969.

Siegfried SASSOON (1886–1967), like Owen and Rosenberg, was shaken into the writing of poetry by his experiences in the trenches in the First World War. He became more famous for his semi-autobiographical prose accounts of the war than for his poetry, although he continued to write verse until late in life.

William SHAKESPEARE (1564–1616) is the greatest figure in English literature and, in many ways, the formulator of the English language as it is today. His thirty-seven plays are constantly staged, studied and analysed, and his 154 sonnets are probably the most famous in the language.

Franz STEINER (1909–1952) was a Czechoslovak exile who became a lecturer in Social Anthropology at Oxford University. He was also well known as a poet.

Cat STEVENS (born 1948). Born in London of Greek Cypriot parents, he had great success in the late 1960s and early 1970s with such songs as 'Matthew and Son' and 'Morning Has Broken', and albums such as 'Tea for the Tillerman' (from which 'Father and Son' (1970) is taken) and 'Foreigner'. Later he became a Moslem and took the name Yusuf Islam.

Alfred, Lord TENNYSON (1809–1882). Considered the greatest poet of the Victorian Age in his own time, especially for the commemorative work *In Memoriam* (1850) which won him the poet laureateship, his reputation declined in the present century. His work is now being re-evaluated and he can be seen in *Idylls of the King* (1859) and many of his late lyrics (of which *Ulysses* is one) as showing a combination of sentiment with deep understanding of the contradictions of his age.

Dylan THOMAS (1914–1953). Born in Swansea, South Wales, Thomas was regarded in his lifetime as one of the finest poets of his generation, his works often being considered a counterpoint to Auden's more politically committed writing. Rhythmically he was a great innovator, although his work can sometimes be criticised for obscurity.

THUCYDIDES (c.460/455–c.399 B.C.) was the most famous historian in classical Greece, writer of a *History of the Peloponnesian War* in eight volumes.

Peter TINNISWOOD (born 1936) is a northerner who worked as a teacher before becoming a journalist, and the writer of several comic novels of northern life which have become famous on British television. *I Didn't Know You Cared* was published in 1973.

Arnold WESKER (born 1932) became famous for his trilogy of plays based on the semi-autobiographical story of a Jewish family in the East end of London – *Chicken Soup with Barley* (1958), *Roots* (1959), and *I'm Talking About Jerusalem* (1960) – which established him as one of the great realistic dramatists of his day. His later work, politically very committed, has been less successful although some of his plays have deserved greater notice.

Oscar WILDE (1854–1900) was the greatest wit of his generation, still well known for his novel *The Picture of Dorian Gray* (1891), many of his short stories and, of course, his classic comedies, the best known of which is *The Importance of Being Earnest* (1895).